The Lives of
Ten Influential
Irishwomen

Clive Scoular

Published in 2009 by
Clive Scoular
Killyleagh
County Down

The author gratefully acknowledges the assistance given unstintingly by his partner, Thomas Johnston, on the layout and design of the book as well as the graphic work undertaken by Sean Doran. Without their willing help, the book would never have been completed.

ISBN 978-0-9539601-7-0

For the unsung women of Ireland

Also by the same author:

James Chichester-Clark, Prime Minister of Northern Ireland

In the Headlines — the Story of the Belfast Europa Hotel

Maeve de Markievicz, Daughter of Constance

John M. Andrews, Northern Ireland's Wartime Prime Minister

Six Famous Sons of Killyleagh

Contents

Introduction 6

Sarah Purser, *Doughty Doyenne* 8

Augusta Gregory, *Passionate Playwright* 20

Alice Milligan, *Plucky Poetess* 34

Maud Gonne, *Reckless Romantic* 46

Constance Markievicz, *Feisty Firebrand* 62

Hanna Sheehy Skeffington, *Steadfast Suffragette* 78

Edith Londonderry, *Cosmopolitan Campaigner* 90

Hazel Lavery, *Spirited Socialite* 100

Mary Bailey, *Audacious Aviatrix* 114

Saidie Patterson, *Courageous Champion* 124

Introduction

For years now I have been researching the lives of many Irishwomen of the 19th and 20th centuries who have generously contributed to Ireland's turbulent yet fascinating history. I have had many opportunities of sharing this information with groups of people of all ages at historical societies, men's and women's groups and in schools. All who have listened to me have made the same comment after hearing their exciting and interesting stories – 'Why have I never heard of this woman before?

Some of my subjects, like Constance Markievicz and Maud Gonne, whilst not exactly household names, will at least be recognised. But what about the others about whom I have written? Who could fail to be proud of Belfast's own Saidie Patterson in her tough, but ultimately successful, fight for women's rights in the vast mills of the city? The poetry of Alice Milligan was powerful and popular and she was reckoned by many to have been Ireland's greatest poet of her day and generation. But have you ever heard of her?

What then of the tenacity of Sarah Purser in ensuring that the skills of Irish painters and stained glass window artists were brought to the fore. Can anyone truly believe that Mary Bailey was altogether wise to take to the air in her flimsy aeroplane in the 1920s with only rudimentary maps and navigation aids and still be the first woman to reach Cape Town?

Hanna Sheehy Skeffington fought for the vote for women in an age not given to offering women any equal opportunities. Edith Londonderry, though titled and wealthy, shone like a beacon in giving help and succour to those who needed it during the difficult days of two world wars. Whilst most readers will know the name of WB Yeats, few will appreciate that it was the patience and endurance of Augusta Gregory which steered him in the right direction, help which sadly he never fully acknowledged. And how much do we owe to the vivacious Hazel Lavery, wife of the renowned Belfast born artist, John Lavery, who used her influence with Michael Collins to accept the Treaty that brought independence to 26 of Ireland's counties in 1921?

Both Maud Gonne and Constance Markievicz were towering women who fought their corners against all odds – and won. Regardless of their privileged upbringing, these two women rolled up their sleeves during difficult times such as the 1913 'Lock Out' to feed the needy and they certainly never rested on their laurels.

It is therefore my intention to encourage everyone to read these stories. They are short enough to give a flavour of the lives of unsung women whose contribution to Ireland was great but yet whose names are largely forgotten. This may now be the opportune time for my readers to take up the full biographies of these exciting women which information I have appended at the end of each story. It is my fervent belief that people in every part of Ireland, both north and south, should know more about these women and be proud of their undoubted achievements. We should perhaps take to heart a phrase I often use, and sincerely mean, - Ireland's women did while Ireland's men merely talked. You may also agree with my sentiment that we in Ireland should at last begin to honour these women living, as we do, in a country not given to honouring its women.

Clive Scoular
Killyleagh, October 2009

Sarah Purser

Doughty Doyenne

Sarah Henrietta Purser was born in Kingstown (modern day Dun Laoghaire) on 22 March 1848, the eighth child and second daughter of Ben and Anne Purser. The Pursers had an interesting pedigree.

Benjamin Purser was born in the year of Trafalgar, 1815, and in 1836, aged just 21, he married Anne Mallet. Neither of their names was particularly Irish although both families, and each nonconformist ones to boot, had been in Ireland for a considerable time. Both came from wealthy stock and were well connected in Dublin's commercial circles. The Pursers had a claim to fame for which they never seem to have been recognised. They were brewers who were the original makers of 'porter'. There were links – not always very cordial ones it has to be said - with the Guinness family but it was the Pursers who came up with 'the black stuff' before the much more celebrated Guinnesses. Be that as it may, it is Guinness that the Irish drink today and not Purser.

Anne Mallet came from an equally well-to-do family who were of Huguenot extraction. Many French Protestants came to Ireland in the 17th century after their expulsion from France in the wake of the St Valentine's Day massacre. They were hard working people who brought prosperity to many towns in Ireland, not least, of course, to Dublin. The Mallets were in the metal foundry business and made good profits and employed many men from different parts of the metropolis.

When Ben proposed to Anne, he was himself working as a clerk for Guinness for a meagre £150 per annum. He decided to resign and, with financial backing from his father, he set up a brewery of his own. But by 1838 it had failed and with an ever growing family he needed a job. He moved with his wife and children to Clonmel in county Cork where he was appointed brewer for Messrs Murphy of Clonmel. He kept this post until 1847 but was never happy there.

Now he moved to Dungarvan in county Waterford in 1848 not long after Sarah's birth. This was an inauspicious year for Ireland. The country was in the midst of the Great Famine which was having a devastating effect on the entire population of Ireland. His family managed to escape the worst ravages of the disease and starvation although for a time it was touch and go. In the same year there was the abortive Young Irelanders' Rebellion which added to the despair of the entire country. Ben and Anne by now had eight children, two daughters and six sons. The entrepreneur Ben, casting aside his pretensions in brewing, made yet another change of occupation and opened a flour mill. This time the venture flourished and, for the next 12 years or so, he made progress in this business. In 1860 however he decided to open another brewery, which precipitated a disastrous decline in his financial fortunes.

There was clearly sufficient money in the family because all ten children (two more boys were born after Sarah) were well educated and all eight sons were sent to Portora Royal School in faraway Enniskillen in county Fermanagh. Sarah and Frances were sent to far off Switzerland, to the Moravian school at Montmirail, for their learning. There they became proficient in French and had also a good command of both Italian and German, all three languages being spoken in different parts of their adopted country. And it was here, in those quiet classrooms in central Europe, that Sarah took her first steps in what was to become her chosen profession. She picked up a paint box and became a very creditable painter. She took a keen interest in her pastime and obviously enjoyed what she was doing. Aged 15, Sarah returned to her home in Dungarvan and for a few years little was heard of her.

On the other hand, unfortunately, much more was heard of Ben Purser. By the early 1870s, his businesses were in decline and he was only saved from bankruptcy with the financial help from other members of his extended family. These various strains on their long and cordial marriage eventually led Ben and Anne to separate. They took their different paths in 1876 after 40 years together. This break in the family greatly affected many of their offspring, not least Sarah. Ben went to live in South Carolina in the United States whilst Anne moved back to Dublin to take up residence at 19 Wellington Road. Sarah, by then 28 years old, went to live with her mother. By now most of her brothers and sisters had gone their diverse ways. It seemed a sad end to this large and vibrant family unit.

Sarah's first steps in her chosen career

The long and successful art career of Sarah Purser started most propitiously. By her early 20s four of her paintings were hung in an exhibition in the Royal Hibernian Academy in 1872. For a young 24 year old woman to be chosen to hang this number of paintings in the male dominated art world in such a similarly dominated city was indeed a great achievement. The men were not given to accepting works by women. They must have been impressed for this became a regular occurrence. Sarah Purser's works were always on show and were universally well received. Sarah then made another courageous decision. Having learnt as much as she felt she could in Dublin, she headed off to Paris to further her art studies at the world famous Academie Julian. There she honed her skills whilst at the same time having the wonderful opportunity to mix with the famous impressionists of the day – Monet, Manet and Whistler to name but a few. She made friends easily and a particular companion of those days was Louise Breslau who was to become a lifelong friend and correspondent. This time spent in the lively atmosphere of the Left Bank and in the art studios of the great painters of the time, served Sarah well in her later life. Her stay in Paris had been a singular success.

After six months Sarah returned to Dublin. It was a wise decision. Her chief interest was portraiture, a genre which, in itself, tended to be rather neglected by Irish artists. This was a shrewd move on Sarah's part and it was not long before she was being pursued to accept commissions. At this time in Ireland there were, of course, many Big Houses with countless members of the landed gentry who had plenty of money to spare for their various family members to sit for portraits. By dint of some useful connections in Dublin and her friendship with Jane L'Estrange,

Sarah was introduced to many influential patrons. The Gore-Booths of Lissadell in county Sligo were relatives of Jane and here Sarah clinched her first residential commission. She painted the two elder daughters of Sir Henry and Lady Georgina, Constance and Eva, as well as their parents. This painting of the young Gore-Booth girls became one of the best known portraits in the whole of Ireland for succeeding generations. And Sarah was being paid handsomely for her work, perhaps earning as much as 60 guineas, a not inconsiderable sum in those days.

The art scene in Dublin in the late 19th century
Even now that Sarah had successfully launched herself into her painting career, she still had time to involve herself in the local art scene. Ireland was soon to become much more aware of its own indigenous talents with the advent of the Irish theatre and Gaelic culture and it could well be said that Sarah Purser did a great deal to promote this image. She was exhibiting not only in the Royal Hibernian Academy but she was also supporting the Irish Fine Arts Club and the Dublin Sketching Club. They were pleased to show her works since she had become by then one of Ireland's finest painters. It was seen as something of a coup for her to be exhibiting with their less illustrious but nonetheless extremely keen members. From all this exposure to the public eye, Sarah was attracting many new customers. She was a prolific artist who had a great empathy with children and she painted many of her young relatives much to their delight. Her pictures were modern and bright and her career was thriving.

In Dublin there were, naturally enough, many more fine artists. Most were men of course and yet it was this almost lonely figure of Sarah Purser who was encouraging these men to display their work. Artists such as Nathaniel Hone and JB Yeats were amongst the nation's finest and most influential painters and they were happy to have Sarah as their friend and mentor.

She now took a studio of her own at 2 Leinster Street. She could afford it with the continuous flow of commissions coming her way. It was de rigueur for the great and good of Dublin to have their portraits painted by Miss Purser. When she was not busy with work in the capital, Sarah would take herself off to Paris to meet her friends and soak up the atmosphere by the banks of the Seine. It also allowed her time to charge her batteries.

But all in the Dublin art garden was not rosy. She might be an artist in demand but she was still a woman and she continued to fight her battles with the misogynists in the city's art world. Sarah was particularly peeved when her younger cousin, Walter Osborne, was appointed an associate of the Royal Hibernian Academy although he had never come close in the number of works he had exhibited with them compared to Sarah. The problem was simple. Sarah was a woman and no matter how good and inventive she was, she was considered as something a little lower than the angels, the male ones of course. She continued to be extremely busy yet she had time to assist the Dublin Fine Arts Club with the administration of their events. It seemed perfectly clear that, if help was needed, then Miss Purser would surely oblige.

By 1884 she had her first painting accepted by one of the world's most prestigious organisations, the Royal Academy in London. She was now certainly in the highest rank of world painters. Yet her local Academy had still not seen fit to elevate her to their hallowed ranks of associate Academicians - and they were not to do so for some time.

Sarah Purser – friend of Ireland
By the late 1880s Sarah had moved her studio to 11 Harcourt Terrace which was a very convenient location near the city centre and also a most comfortable house. She now entered a new phase in her life. Having made the acquaintance of all the prominent artists in Dublin she now decided to widen her circle of friends. Sarah has been described as having 'an insatiable appetite for discussion'. So she started to invite all kinds and conditions of men and women to her house, there, as she said, to have their wits sharpened. Generous to a fault, she showered gifts upon her friends, and it was soon an honour to be invited to one of Miss Purser's afternoon salons where they would engage in debates with the others who had also received invitations. Amongst those to visit were WB Yeats, AE (George Russell), Douglas Hyde (the founder of the Gaelic League and, in 1938, to become the first President of Ireland) and Stephen Gwynn. In later years at the beginning of the 20th century many from conflicting camps in nationalist and unionist Ireland accepted invitations to Miss Purser's in the full knowledge that their political opponents would be present. It could well have been the case that, by meeting in these comfortable surroundings, they felt more confident to converse with one another.

Sarah continued to visit Paris to renew her acquaintances with those she knew there and also to share in their joys and sorrows. On one of these visits to the French capital she met Maud Gonne and her lover, and father of her two illegitimate children, Lucien Millevoye. She painted a portrait of Maud, a painting with is regularly seen to this day and which adorns the cover of Maud's rather incomplete autobiography *Servant of the Queen*.

Back in London she accepted a commission to paint a portrait of the Land League champion, Michael Davitt. Then, in contrast, she painted the likeness of Viscount Castlereagh, later to become the 7th Marquis of Londonderry, husband of the elegant hostess, Edith, and also the first Minister of Education in James Craig's Northern Ireland government. Fees for these works were lucrative and Sarah had little to worry about on the financial front.

By this time in her private life Sarah was living with her mother and during this period she was to suffer the sadness of the death of her only sister, Frances, in 1890.

Ireland's leading portraitist

Sarah was, by 1890, the undisputed number one portraitist in Ireland. Somewhat grudgingly, one imagines, the committee of the Royal Hibernian Academy agreed to install Sarah as an Honorary Academician at the age of 42. She accepted the plaudits from an adoring art public and perhaps a rather more restrained accolade from the Academy. But she was pleased and accepted the honour with pride and dignity. Soon she was off to Belfast to exhibit some of her paintings there. Her fame had spread throughout the land and the northerners were delighted that such an artist as Sarah should come to their city.

Her diary was ever more and more full. She renewed her friendship with Douglas Hyde and commended the work he was doing in his Gaelic League. After all Irish painters would surely benefit from the League's determination that local artists should take a more prominent place in Irish society.

In 1893 she exhibited no fewer than eight works in the Royal Hibernian Academy's annual show. There were paintings there, of course, of her main competitors. Hone, Yeats and Osborne were forever vying with Sarah for the honour of being the top artist in Ireland. There was no contest yet she always praised work undertaken by these fine artists. Through her influence a committee of artists in Dublin was able to attract a feast of impressionist works by the famed Corot, Manet, Whistler, Degas and Monet for a special exhibition in Dublin in 1898. It was, needless to say, a huge success, much of it due to the fact that Dublin's very own Sarah Purser knew these men herself and was able to influence them into bringing their works to the Irish capital.

The turn of the century

By 1900 Sarah was 52 years old and she had the almost total care of her mother who had become unwell and needed constant attention. Her father, who had emigrated to America over 20 years previously, had recently died and one of Sarah's brothers was ill. Mrs Purser died in 1901 but, by this time and owing to these more personal burdens being placed upon her, Sarah had of necessity to scale down the number of commissions which she felt able to accept. In order to revive her strength Sarah set off on a long vacation to the Levant early in 1902. She greatly benefited from the holiday and returned to Dublin ready to pick up her paint brushes once more. Within a few months of her return, however, she was to suffer another family bereavement. Her younger artist cousin, Walter Osborne, died in April 1903 leaving Sarah as the sole torch bearer for the painters in the family connection.

Everyone in society, from the greatest artist and highest nobility to the fine ordinary citizens of Dublin, knew the name Sarah Purser. They were proud of her and of her achievements for Dublin in particular and Ireland in general. She was a true and worthy public figure. She had made her mark. Now she was to further her fame and reputation. Her greatest challenge was now set before her.

An Tur Gloine – the Tower of Glass

By the turn of the century more and more Irish people were showing a true interest in Ireland's native skills, sports and crafts. For too long Ireland's artistic riches of earlier centuries had been lost and little or no consideration was being given to trying to revive these traditions. Sarah Purser was to the fore in doing something about making the Irish proud of their ancient crafts. The Roman Catholic church, having at last broken free of the established Church of Ireland in 1869, was building numerous churches and cathedrals. The hierarchy throughout the land, from Cork to Cavan and from Westport to Dublin, were dispensing their new-found largesse and appointing all sorts of artisans to build and adorn their wonderful new edifices. However, in their enthusiasm to make their new houses of worship even more spectacular than any other cathedral in the country, they forgot one important aspect. In their zeal to employ the very best sculptors, designers and painters, they overlooked local Irish talent. They brought in craftsmen from every part of Europe, from Germany and France and from Spain to Italy to beautify these new churches. They seemed to ignore native talent or perhaps they did not even consider that such existed.

There then entered the fray, so to speak, not some great Catholic theologian or thinker, but the nonconformist Sarah Purser. She could not believe that the Irish themselves could not provide the skills needed to adorn their own churches. So she simply approached the Catholic bishops and archbishops in their palaces and put it to them that if they could not find native talent then she would. She saw a particular niche where she felt she could help. Stained glass windows form a central and integral part of any church and are usually the first sight to behold. The bishops, hearing the enthusiasm of this formidable lady, who was not even one of their own flock to boot, felt abashed and maybe somewhat shame-faced. They had to admit to their own shortcomings and listened carefully to what Miss Purser had to say to them. They were soon to be very content that they had taken the time to be advised by Sarah.

She then set about setting up a factory which could supply the requisite artefacts. With the help of an Irish MP, TP Gill, who proposed instituting stained glass window classes in Dublin, and the patronage of Edward Martyn, an influential Catholic member of the gentry from county Galway, the scheme quickly transformed from a vague idea into a firm resolve. She instinctively felt that there were Irish artisans who could surely do better than the continentals who had, at least in Sarah's opinion, failed to do the new buildings justice. She was particularly unimpressed at the embellishments in the new Catholic cathedral in Thurles, county Tipperary, and, having viewed many portraits of the members of the Catholic hierarchy painted by mediocre European artists, she lashed out at Irish painters for spending too much time painting landscapes and ignoring the opportunities to paint portraits.

Being a woman of her word Sarah set about financing and finding a suitable location for her Tower of Glass. The first people she needed were experts in the field of stained glass. In Dublin she engaged the services of Alfred E Child, a student of the great English specialist, Christopher Whall. Premises were located at 24 Upper Pembroke Street close to Leeson Street and relatively near Dublin city centre. She appreciated that she would need to provide the money to finance the project and this she gladly did. It took over 20 years for her to be recompensed for her outgoings. But this did not concern Sarah Purser. She had successfully found her workshop and artists to undertake this great challenge. 'An Tur Gloine' was ready to launch on 1 January 1903.

By this early stage Sarah had already been involved in what was probably their first commission. In 1901 she had had discussions with the clergy designing the new Catholic cathedral in Loughrea, county Galway to be dedicated to St Brendan. Of all the outstanding work carried out over quarter of a century by the team at the Tower, the glorious windows in St Brendan's stand out even to this day. Sarah had herself no skills in making stained glass and so she went about learning them. Whilst the bulk of the work at St Brendan's was carried out by Alfred Child and his disciple, Irishman Michael Healy, Sarah did herself produce one exquisite little window in the porch of the cathedral. But Sarah realised that she had to give the artists their head to get on with the work and she was rarely to be disappointed with the result. Their flair for this genre was exceptional and to view their work became the chief delight of that and succeeding generations.

As the years went by Sarah was able to attract the best stained glass artists in the land. Many of them were women like Evie Hone, Ethel Rhind, Beatrice Elvery (later to become Lady Glenavy), Kitty O'Brien and Wilhelmina Geddes. During the first 25 years of its existence, the Tower of Glass completed no fewer than 637 commissions, most of them in Ireland. By dint of her drive and determination Sarah Purser, almost single-handedly, had shown the world that Irish stained glass painters and producers were second to none. Their work is a living confirmation of this assertion.

Sir Hugh Lane
Now that the Tower was firmly on its feet with countless orders coming in, Sarah felt able to leave much of the work there to her team of fine artists. She turned her attention once more to undertaking more commissions for portraits and soon they were flooding in. At the same time she showed an amount of compassion by organising an exhibition for two of her friends, the artists Nathaniel Hone and Jack B Yeats. These men were most accomplished painters but they had struggled in recent times to promote their work. They needed an impetus and that came in the guise of Sarah Purser. She set about organising a showing of these men's works in Dublin city centre and the outcome was a great success. Hone and Yeats immediately became much more in demand and they expressed their gratitude to

Sarah for the tangible help she had given to put their works more prominently in the public eye. This was the kind of woman she was. She would not shrink from giving assistance where and when she could.

As luck would have it yet another saviour rode in on his white charger to give Hone and Yeats a further boost. This came in the form of the wealthy and distinguished art dealer, Sir Hugh Lane. He had been born in 1875 and was a nephew of the Irish playwright, Lady Augusta Gregory. By visiting the exhibition and renewing his acquaintance with Sarah, Hugh Lane had enhanced, by his very presence, the work of these two struggling artists. He was becoming a regular visitor to Dublin because he wanted to create a municipal art gallery in the city to enable its citizens to enjoy works of art. This particular scheme, and its consequences, was to run through Irish life for the next century right up to the present day. Lane and Dublin Corporation never seemed to be able to come to agreement over the location for, and the money to fund, this gallery. By 1908, however, some progress on the scheme had been made. Temporary premises were provided and the gallery became a reality.

Sarah was lukewarm in her support yet she generously set aside her doubts and endorsed the venture. Hugh Lane fought hard to turn the temporary gallery into a permanent one and one which would do justice to the great city of Dublin. He was a remarkable man whose tenacity, or stubbornness, depending on how people saw him, was to be his downfall. After six long years there was still no agreement for the splendid gallery he had in mind. In 1913 he approached the famous English architect Sir Edwin Lutyens to come up with a plan. The design was, in the eyes of most Dublin people, quite outrageous. He planned to build an ambitious edifice across the river Liffey in the middle of the city. Now at last did the city fathers stop humming and hawing. They refused to countenance such a hare-brained scheme. An impasse had been reached; further progress seemed unlikely.

The central purpose for the gallery was to find a home for 39 masterpieces which Lane wanted to bequeath to a new Dublin municipal gallery. These paintings, by impressionists like Manet and Degas, were both valuable and truly outstanding. To have these works as the centrepiece in a gallery in Dublin would have made it the envy of galleries all over the world. Lane had, after all, made his fortune by having been able to pick up all sorts of works of art for rock bottom prices (it was even rumoured that he had bought a Gainsborough in his early days for £10). He now wanted Dublin to benefit from his generosity but its city fathers seemed unwilling to cooperate with him. He huffed and puffed and threatened to leave them to the National Gallery in London. But deep down he wanted the pictures to have a home in Dublin and he ensured that his will mirrored his aspiration. Consequently he drew up a further codicil to his will so that they would remain on Irish shores in the event of his death. Fate was then to deal a mighty blow to his plans. Returning from America in 1915 not long after the outbreak of the First World War, his ship, the *Lusitania*, was torpedoed off the Cork coast and sank with heavy loss of life. Amongst the dead was Sir Hugh Lane. His family grieved his loss made worse by the fact that his body was never found.

For the art world the loss of Hugh Lane was devastating. At least they consoled themselves in the knowledge that his wonderful paintings would be a constant reminder of the man's kindness in a Dublin gallery. Not so, they soon discovered. Hugh Lane, careful and conscientious man that he had been, had actually forgotten to have that final codicil to his will properly witnessed. In effect this meant that the 39 paintings would go to London and not remain in Dublin as everyone knew was the desire of Lane himself. And so it has been this oversight of Hugh Lane's that has remained an absolute nightmare for the art world ever since.

Sarah Purser to the rescue

The denizens of the art world in Dublin now turned to the inimitable Miss Purser to see if she could help unravel this calamity. Hugh Lane's aunt, Lady Augusta Gregory, was of course also involved. For both these elderly ladies (Sarah was by now 67 and her friend, Lady Gregory 63) the task was a formidable one. They knew the clear intentions of Hugh; he wished for the paintings to be displayed in Dublin. The art dealers and artists agreed that this was his wish; the people of Dublin hoped that they would stay for them to continue to admire them in their own city. But the lawyers had a different idea. Although they may have agreed that Lane had wanted the pictures to stay in Dublin, his will had not been so endorsed. The codicil had been unfortunately left unwitnessed and the extant will had donated them to the National Gallery in London. For months and years the ladies continued to struggle to have Hugh's clear intention accepted. The paintings remained in London and, although they were from time to time brought over to Dublin for short exhibitions, they stayed firmly in London. Not even the strenuous endeavours of the doughty Miss Purser could change the situation. Her aim may have been very clear but those in charge, with their legal rights assured, baulked Sarah for the rest of her life.

Sarah Purser may not have been able to resolve this tricky matter but she was, nonetheless, still loved and appreciated in the Irish art world. She accepted a seat on the Board of the National Gallery of Ireland and continued to please many clients with her delightful portraits of members of their families. She even bought a motor car as far back as 1913 and this enabled her to get out into the countryside where she had taken an interest in painting landscapes.

The problem surrounding the future of Hugh Lane's paintings was not the only tragedy to occur during the war. By now Sarah was living with her eldest brother in Mespil House, a mansion set in five acres of ground again close to the city centre. She continued to meet many of the figures involved in art and politics at her salon discussions each week. Sarah was not the archetypal 'head in the clouds' artist. She fully appreciated the state of the world and the horrors it was going through in those years. She also, and more importantly, understood, as well as anyone could, the tragedies absorbing her own Ireland. She knew the fears of the people of every opinion as well as the significance of the Home Rule crisis. She did her best to bring together the 'warring' factions and, where others fled the city, Sarah remained to give what advice and assistance she could.

In April 1916 the Easter Rising broke out and she was in Dublin during those fateful days. She knew many of those involved and even some of those who were executed after the events. She was devastated to discover that the Royal Hibernian Academy had been burned down during the bombardment of the city centre. Inside countless priceless Irish paintings were lost – and lost forever. Included were eight of the finest paintings of Sarah Purser. Whilst everyone knows something of the Rising and the fact that the General Post Office was burnt out few realise that Ireland's most precious art works were lost as well.

The twilight years

Sarah remained in Dublin through all those momentous years for Ireland, 1916-1923. When the cruel Civil War ended in 1923 Sarah was at last acknowledged by the Royal Hibernian Academy. They made her an associate Academician. She was now 75 years old and had contributed to Ireland's artistic renascence for over half a century. And so the men decided that this extraordinary woman could become an associate of their esteemed school of art. They then, just to prove that they were open to further concessions, made her an Academician the next year, 1924. Sarah had achieved greatness even in the eyes of that male dominated academy. However she bore no grudges and accepted the accolade with her usual aplomb.

She was still painting and organising exhibitions, mainly to give up-and-coming artists a boost. In 1928 her Tower of Glass celebrated its silver anniversary and nothing pleased her more at its worthwhile achievements. She was a proud woman and lauded throughout the land. Whilst continuing the unequal struggle to resolve the future of the 39 paintings of Hugh Lane's, she was delighted to hear that the Dublin Corporation had donated Charlemont House as a permanent site for their municipal gallery. It opened to the public, for whom it had after all been gifted, in 1933. There was much satisfaction that this stage had at last been reached. Sarah felt she could now retire.

In 1938 the art establishment of Ireland and further afield honoured Sarah by putting on a wonderful 90th birthday celebration. Those attending, and most of them of generations younger than hers, had the chance to shake her hand and thank her for her enduring commitment to the arts in Ireland.

In her later years she enjoyed travelling through Europe, especially France and Italy and to renewing friendships she had made in her early life. She suffered a stroke in the first days of August 1943 and died on 7 August, at the grand old age of 95. Her work for Ireland is enduring but the question remains whether anyone today remembers the legacy she left for Ireland.

Suggested reading
1.   Coxhead, Elizabeth, *Daughters of Erin – Five Women of the Irish Renascence*, London, 1965.
2.   O'Grady, John, *The Life and Work of Sarah Purser*, Dublin, 1996.

Augusta Gregory

Passionate Playwright

Dudley Persse of Roxborough, county Galway, was the father of Isabella Augusta, born on 15 March 1852. Augusta was her father's 12th child. He had been married twice, his first wife dying young after having borne him his first three children. He then married Frances Barry of the artistic and cultured O'Grady family and she bore him a further thirteen children. He was, therefore, the father of sixteen children. Large families born to the gentry were not at all uncommon during the 19th century although such a very large number was a little out of the ordinary.

Roxborough was an imposing three storey castellated house not very far from the town of Loughrea, a few miles from Galway city. The family, like most of the landed families throughout Ireland, employed many servants and so the children were well looked after. Augusta, born not long after the end of the Great Famine, was educated at home, like all her sisters, by various governesses, most of them willing but sadly not up to the job. Her brothers had their tutors and this meant that for most of their young lives the Persse children enjoyed each other's company throughout their formative years. When they came of age the girls would usually find a husband amongst the neighbouring gentry and the boys were sent off to win fame and fortune, and a wife, further afield. This was the accepted practice of the time but for this Persse generation, things did not work out exactly according to plan.

Augusta's marriage

Augusta, by the age of 27, had still not found a husband and was considered to be firmly 'on the shelf'. This did not overly concern her as she had plenty to do in looking after the needs of the tenants. She enjoyed reading to them, assisting their children and even writing letters on behalf of the workers of the estate. But, in 1880, she was sent off to the south of France to look after one of her older brothers, Richard, who was ill. There she met, although not for the first time, Sir William Gregory, a 63-year-old widower who was returning from Ceylon (today Sri Lanka) where he had been governor.

Sir William's was a fascinating history. He had been born in July 1817 in Dublin to another wealthy Galway family whose stately home was Coole Park near Gort, close neighbours of the Persses at Roxborough. One of William's ancestors had, in his early life, stowed away to India where he made good and eventually became chairman of the great East India Company. With the money he made he was able to build up the Coole Park estate.

William went to school at Harrow and, although a bright boy, he did not progress to university but went into Parliament instead. He represented a Dublin seat for a few years in the 1840s and there became friendly with Daniel O'Connell. He then gave up his parliamentary seat and returned to Coole Park on the death of his father. His major failing was his love of horse racing and he lost so much money that he had to sell part of the estate to pay off his debts. This was certainly an inauspicious start for the new squire of Coole Park. But he was able to redeem himself and went back to Westminster as MP for Galway in 1857 where he not only supported Catholic emancipation, but also championed the demands of tenants to own the land. Neither of these campaigns brought him many friends from within establishment circles.

In 1872 he married a wealthy young widow, Elizabeth Bowdoin, and sailed with her to Ceylon where he had been appointed governor. He was a popular administrator who improved the lot of the islanders in many aspects of their lives. But the fates were against him when his wife took ill and died less than two years after their marriage. Island life in the Far East had not appealed to her and she simply gave up the will to live.

William Gregory, heartbroken, set sail to return home and it was when his ship stopped off in the south of France that he renewed his neighbourly acquaintance with Augusta Persse who was there looking after her brother, Richard. A romance blossomed and the couple soon became engaged. They married in Dublin on 4 March 1880. After their marriage they went back to Ceylon and India and, for most of the years of their years together, Augusta saw much of the world. They only ever stayed at their Coole Park home for the summer each year although a few weeks were also spent at their London home. In May 1881, their son, Robert, was born. He was to be the couple's only child. The baby was looked after by nannies whilst his parents visited their many friends throughout Europe. It was during these perambulations that Augusta fell in love with the wealthy English poet, Wilfrid Scawen Blunt. Their affair lasted only for a short time and it was fairly certain that her husband knew of the liaison. This was the only period in Augusta's life when she felt wanted, not just as a raconteuse and bonne vivante, but as a woman. Soon the Gregorys were spending as much time as they could at Coole Park for it was less expensive to live there than at their London home. And, at last, Augusta had the opportunity to get to know her son.

Coole Park

When, at last, Augusta got the chance to spend time at her new home, she was delighted and entranced. She grew quickly to love the place with its spacious rooms, well-stocked libraries and enchanting gardens. She was also very popular with the tenants and the local people. Everyone realised that Lady Gregory was on the side of her people which meant that, even during the excesses of the Land Leaguers (who were doing their best to grab land, mostly from the gentry), Coole Park was spared the attacks and destruction brought upon many of their neighbours' grand houses. More importantly too, in later and even more disturbed times during the War of Independence and the Civil War, the house was never violated. The reason for this was the attitude, presence and empathy of Lady Gregory.

Augusta Gregory – playwright and author

It was not long after her marriage that Augusta found her true vocation. She had discovered her life's work. She took to writing plays and encouraging others to do so. From being a rather diffident young woman she soon became much more confident and self-assured. Her guests were invariably those of a similar bent to herself. She had a copper beech tree in the garden which became known as the 'Visitors' Book' or 'Autograph' tree. She only invited her favourite literary friends to sign it whilst others were merely taken to see it. Nonetheless the tree remains to this day, even if the house itself does not. From this point on in her life Coole Park became a place of refuge and a place of peace and tranquillity. She just loved having like-minded guests staying with her and the house was rarely empty.

Life soon changed when, in 1892 just before her 40th birthday, her husband died aged 75. William had had a most happy, if late, marriage and had left Coole Park in good hands. Augusta was left comfortably off. She went into mourning and from then on wore black for the rest of her life. She sold the London house and bought a little flat as a bolthole in the capital. But what most pleased her was that she now had no further need to travel all over the world – she could just live her life at her own pace at her beloved Coole Park.

It was at this stage, in the early 1890s, that she surrounded herself with such soon-to-be luminaries as WB Yeats and JM Synge. They often visited Coole Park where they knew that they would not only be welcome but they could also work on their writing and poetry. They knew too that Augusta Gregory was always at hand to listen, discuss and encourage and usually to feed them. The truth of the matter is that she must have often been 'put upon' by these voracious geniuses. Yeats's friendship lasted their entire lives although it is my contention that he got much more out of the relationship than did Augusta. There were many who declared that they were in love but their relationship was more probably just one of mutual affection.

Augusta herself was writing a great many plays which were later to be well considered and regularly performed throughout the country as well as in England and America. She kept her feet firmly on the ground, however, and gave top priority to the educational needs of her son as well as giving generously to any good work being organised in the district. Many of the school parties and village fetes were sponsored and often run by Lady Gregory herself. Her kindness to all her less fortunate neighbours and their children was legendary. A typical image of Augusta Gregory, especially in her later years, was of a group of the neighbours' children arriving at the front door to ask their benefactor if she had any apples or blackcurrants or flowers to spare. They never left empty handed, rather running off home with their pockets stuffed to the brim with produce from the Coole Park garden. Her motto was – what is mine is also theirs. The tenants and locals knew this and were always respectful and thankful for her generosity.

An Irish literary renascence

Augusta Gregory not only spent time writing; she also spent a great deal of time learning the Irish language and understanding the ways of the rural Irish. She loved to collect folk lore which meant that she spent time with the poor people themselves in their cottages. She loved to be steeped in their story telling sessions and, on more than one occasion, visited the people of Inishmaan, the middle of the Aran islands off the Galway coast. These experiences enabled her to write truly authentic plays which soon graced the theatre stages throughout Ireland.

It was at the nearby Tullira home of her Catholic gentry neighbour, Edward Martyn, that the first discussion took place concerning the founding of a national theatre. With the support of such eminent people as Douglas Hyde, soon to found the Gaelic League in 1893, as well as Yeats and Synge, the proposal seemed worth pursuing. Augusta was the budding playwright and Yeats and his contemporaries the talented poets and writers. This seemed the opportune time to proceed with this plan. Ireland had, during the latter years of the 19th century, been throwing off the shackles of the establishment and building up and reviving the artistic skills of the native Irish themselves. It was time to support home talents. For too long the English had been coming to Dublin to perform and it was now time to encourage and engage local actors and actresses for a truly Irish theatre. The new Abbey Theatre was born with fine actors such as the Fay brothers, William and Frank, being given the chance to perform in a decent and well-appointed playhouse rather than in the dingy back street halls where they previously had to ply their trade.

For the ten years after 1902 and the re-emergence of the Irish theatre, Augusta Gregory was at the peak of her writing. Her best plays were being written and performed to adoring audiences, delighted at last to savour genuine Irish talent. Occasionally Augusta had to tread the boards herself when an actress did not turn up or was ill. She was no slouch as an actress herself but, of course, much preferred her leading ladies like Sara Allgood and Maire O'Neill. Throughout her years at the Abbey Augusta had to walk a fine line between enthralling the masses and keeping in with the moneyed classes. The ordinary people were the bread and butter of the theatre but the upper crust were those with the financial means to keep the theatre afloat. Much of the early funding came from a rich Englishwoman, Annie Horniman. Augusta never really warmed to Miss Horniman but she knew that she had to tolerate her to ensure the necessary funds for the theatre. For years she was successful although some years later, when the theatre had become successful, Annie Horniman left to offer her largesse to a provincial English theatre.

A deepening involvement in the Irish theatre

Now that the new theatre had been opened in Abbey Street in December 1904, opening with Augusta's *Spreading the News*, the triumvirate of Augusta, Synge and Yeats proceeded to enthuse and encourage many native Irish men and women to write plays for their rapidly increasing audiences. They themselves wrote many works for the Abbey and there were always plenty of their offerings enchanting their ever more enthusiastic audiences. The three of them fought amongst themselves from time to time with Augusta usually the one who acted as referee. They were literally living in each other's pockets and undertaking remarkable work in staging plays without having time to enjoy any breaks from their punishing schedule.

The relationship between Yeats and Augusta was a complex one. Basically they were frustrated individuals although their talent was prodigious. Usually Augusta just gave in to Willie in order to concentrate on the work in hand. They remained close their entire lives, even in the midst of the marathon 'on-off' love affair between Maud Gonne and Yeats. In many ways, Augusta was also in love with Yeats, if only in a platonic way.

Augusta and Synge were much more popular with the actors and actresses at the theatre who found Yeats obnoxious and overbearing. When they had complaints, and this was a regular occurrence, they went off to have a private meeting with Augusta to try to resolve their problems. There were times, too, when some of their best staff, both producers and actors, simply could not stand the squabbling anymore and resigned. But Augusta saw this as yet another challenge and overcame it. Every new script had to be read and agreed or altered. And in those days even the paper on which the plays were handwritten was of poor quality. By the first years of the 20th century the Abbey Theatre had truly become a national one and was extremely popular. Funding, it has to be said, was always an ongoing concern, especially when Annie Horniman deserted them. Augusta then used her considerable skill in ensuring subsidies from the government when matters got difficult.

For all those early years of the theatre, a vast burden of work rested on Augusta's shoulders. It must not be forgotten that she did not live in Dublin year round. Her home was at Coole Park in the west in county Galway. For a woman of continuing advancing years, this journey became wearisome. She had to be driven from Coole Park to the railway station in Gort where she travelled for a few miles and alighted at Athenry to await the Dublin train. Often she had a two hour wait in a draughty waiting room although, to be fair to the station staff, they often kept a roaring fire there just for their favourite passenger, Lady Gregory. In Dublin she was usually met by Yeats or Synge or some of her city friends and immediately taken to the theatre. During the long days at the Abbey she rarely went out for a restaurant meal as she did not like dining on her own. She would bring food all the way from Coole and eat that in the theatre. None of this deterred this valiant woman for she thoroughly enjoyed the cut and thrust of theatre life. When there was a special performance, for example, she would bring her wonderful homemade barmbrack and lots of other 'goodies' for the acting staff from Coole Park. The actors and actresses had often at least two performances per day and were much underfed. They were grateful for Augusta's care and attention to them for they could easily have gone hungry without her beneficence.

Robert, Augusta's son, whose heart was not in academia, went off to the Slade Art School in London to learn to paint. He became a very proficient stage set designer and, in later years, he helped his mother with a number of his creations for the performances at the Abbey. Many of these lively sets caused sensations although Augusta was inwardly very pleased with her son's contributions. They seemed to mirror the kind of people the Gregorys were – doughty and defiant.

Strained relations, however, continued to be the order of the day. When the Fay brothers and Miss Horniman wanted an Englishman, Ben Payne, appointed as co-producer, Augusta dug in her heels. The Fays resigned but Augusta and Yeats were not altogether concerned although Augusta, true to form, had to face the unprovoked verbal attacks from these men who should have known better. They soon engaged actors who were every bit as good as the previous ones had been. The Abbey was becoming a magnet for budding performers.

Challenging days for the Abbey
As Augusta continued to write works for the theatre, she and her fellow directors were always looking out for more talent. They knew Douglas Hyde very well. He was an Irish language enthusiast who, in 1893, had formed the Gaelic League. Whilst not a playwright in the strictest terms, he still was a powerful lyricist with lots of brilliant ideas for plays. Consequently Augusta helped him with various scenarios which improved the presentation of his work. Hyde was a natural communicator and did well with Augusta and Yeats. Many of the works he produced were in the Irish language and were just as popular in the theatre as any other in its repertoire. Contributions from Edward Martyn and GB Shaw were added to the Abbey's collection of excellent material.

However when, in January 1907, John Synge's powerful play *The Playboy of the Western World* was performed there were riots in the theatre. Like much of the subject matter of Synge's work, it was too controversial for many of the staid Dublin public. Many of them had blinkered vision and did not accept that what was being performed did actually represent real Irish life. But Augusta (Yeats and Synge conveniently being absent) rode out the storm because she truly believed that this play was one of the best which had ever been written for their theatre. By refusing to give in to pure ignorance meant that *Playboy* eventually became a firm favourite. This was not the first, nor was it to be the last, riotous disturbance in the Abbey but, as the years went on, theatregoers in Dublin finally realised what a wonderful theatre they had in their midst. For Augusta, however, the repercussions of the *Playboy* riots meant the loss of valuable support in her own county Galway; for years she was not forgiven for putting on such a contentious play; for years she was not permitted to help the children in and around Gort as she had done for many years previously. In the end, the rift was healed although it did prove to Augusta how intense feelings become, even in her own beloved county.

When King Edward died in 1910, Augusta and the Abbey got into yet more trouble. Although she had sent a telegram from Coole Park to cancel the performances on that day, it did not arrive in time and the matinee had already started. She was in hot water again and lost considerable support, especially from her Anglo Irish patrons and sponsors. But, as ever, she picked herself up and strode on with her usual determination.

In 1903 Augusta had her portrait painted by Jack Yeats and again in 1906 by Antonio Mancini (who was also responsible for a fine portrait of her nephew, Hugh Lane). Robert, her son, married Margaret Parry, in September 1907. Augusta now felt a degree of family pressure in that she was not any longer the chatelaine of Coole Park, but she hung on and things turned out in her favour as the years went by. She was, of course, delighted when her first grandchild, Richard, was born on 6 January 1909, although there still was that unspoken threat to her position at Coole Park. Not long after the child's birth Augusta suffered a cerebral haemorrhage which nearly killed her although she soon recovered to get on with the many tasks in hand.

The Abbey players visit America

Shortly after the birth of her granddaughter, Anne, in September 1911, Augusta set off by sea a week after the company had departed for the United States. On board ship she wrote one of her best tragedies *MacDonough's Wife*. The Abbey players had been invited to tour and perform many of the plays of Yeats, Synge, Augusta and others. Their fame had gone before them and they proved to be a great hit with huge audiences wherever they went. Augusta herself, having always been a rather diffident person in Ireland and not keen on giving speeches, now found that she loved public speaking. She discovered that she was an accomplished orator and this discovery gave her immense satisfaction. The company travelled from city to city all over the country. The tour was a great success and was favourably reported in the newspapers both in Ireland and in America. During the tour Augusta met President Taft in Washington which was a singular honour for the director of a travelling Irish theatre company.

However there were, just as there had been in Dublin, disturbances at some theatres in New York when *The Playboy of the Western World* was performed. This reminded Augusta that there were Irish hardliners no matter where she went. The trouble did not, however, in any way detract from the enjoyment given by the Abbey Players to their adoring American audiences.

When they returned in triumph to Dublin after almost six months (the tour had been extended by three months owing to its success) Augusta Gregory had reached the zenith of her career. She was more popular and adored than she had ever been previously or would be in the future. And the tour had been extremely financially successful too, something which pleased Augusta and the players and, more so, their administrators and bankers. In the ensuing years the company returned to America on three further occasions but it was probably the first tour which created the best impressions and netted the most money.

Whilst Augusta was in America she met John Quinn, an Irish American with whom she had been corresponding. He was wealthy man who was keen to assist the Abbey and its productions as much as he could. Although he was almost 20 years younger than Augusta, there sprung up a deep affection one for the other. Augusta became very fond of John and was most likely in love with him. They kept in touch and saw each other when the Abbey Players were in America but whether or not they would have ever married is more a matter of conjecture. Augusta may have, to many, appeared staid and unworldly, but remembering her relationships with Wilfrid Blunt, her on-going love for Willie Yeats and now this dalliance with John Quinn, it is certain that Augusta Gregory was a woman of every emotion, not just prim and proper, but also worldly and attracted to men.

The World War, the Easter Rising and the Lane paintings

Throughout her long and complex life Augusta Gregory faced many challenges. Most other people would have buckled under the strain, but not so Lady Gregory. When the First World War broke out, many of her male relatives joined up. Her son, Robert, was one of the first followed by almost a dozen of her many nephews. By the end of that war to end all wars, her clan had lost six gallant young men, seven when we count Robert himself who was killed in the last year of the conflict, 1918. Many Big House families suffered dreadfully and many heirs and younger sons were killed in wars the world over.

But the first challenge revolved around one of her nephews who was not an enlisted man – Hugh Lane, the son of her sister, Adelaide. Born in 1875 in a rather loveless home, Hugh went to London where he soon discovered his forte. He had an uncanny knack in sniffing out, and purchasing cheaply, many valuable paintings and other works of art and was soon a wealthy self-made entrepreneur and art dealer. He had been keen to see a municipal art gallery built in Dublin so that its citizens could view and admire wonderful artefacts. He carried on a fight with Dublin Corporation to encourage them as to the merits of his case. As a sweetener he offered to gift to the new gallery 39 priceless paintings (many by the famous impressionists Degas, Renoir and Picasso as well as many others). These paintings were to become the bane of every government's life for years to come. Lane had eventually agreed to leave the paintings to Dublin although the final site for the gallery had not been established. He signed a codicil to his will which ensured that the works of art would be returned from the National Gallery in London to Dublin. He then headed off to America on business. But then tragedy struck and he was amongst the hundreds who were drowned off the Old Head of Kinsale off the Cork coast when the *Lusitania* was torpedoed by a German U-boat in September 1915.

Augusta Gregory had been named as the sole executrix of Hugh's will and from then on, right until her own death, she was entangled in this most convoluted and tiresome affair. She wrote letters; she cajoled MPs and Prime Ministers; she appealed to everyone she knew to support the case for the immediate return of the Lane paintings to Dublin. The matter stretched on for years. First there was a promise to find them a new home in Dublin and then the London people refused to give way. It is hard, at this distance in time, to even imagine the frustrations and depressions which Augusta endured just to get a hold of these paintings which her nephew clearly meant to be in Dublin. In the end Augusta was unable to satisfactorily resolve the impasses caused by Hugh Lane's carelessness in not having his codicil properly witnessed. It was also left to Augusta to write the biography of Hugh Lane which was received with acclaim when it was published. Few realised the ramifications of all this work on an already hardworking woman who was, by now, well into her sixties.

Then came the awful consequences of the Great War. During the conflict the Abbey continued to put on productions. There were obvious difficulties in finding actors when many were away on the western front but they generally were able to carry on with performances.

The Easter Rising caused disruption for the Abbey; it caused disruption for Ireland in a much greater way. On the opening day of the rebellion, one of the best known Abbey actors, Sean Connolly, was shot dead in an encounter near Dublin Castle. Thus the theatre world had lost one of its own. During that Easter week, the Royal Hibernian Academy was burnt down in the conflagration which enveloped Sackville (later O'Connell) Street towards the end of the rising. Ireland's cultural heritage had also suffered badly in this upheaval.

During the Easter Rising Augusta was at home at Coole Park. It took some time to bring the news of rebels on the streets. She could only wait and see what would become of Dublin in the aftermath of what was, initially at least, an unpopular rebellion. The Abbey survived; the Lane picture squabbles continued; the country careered into yet more mayhem and murder. Soon the War of Independence and the Civil War would wreak havoc, vengeance and destruction upon a country least able to deal with such cruelties.

As Augusta remained at Coole Park looking after her grandchildren she prayed daily that her only son and heir would return to his family and his inheritance. But it was not to be. In January 1918 the news she had dreaded was brought to her door at Coole Park by a retainer whose demeanour immediately indicated to the chatelaine that her son was dead. He had been shot down over Italy by a friendly plane. This surely was the most cruel irony – that your friend had killed you when you were doing your best to save his country. Augusta could hardly bear to tell her daughter-in-law and her grandchildren. The news was received sombrely and sadly. Augusta Gregory then appreciated that she was no longer mistress of Coole Park - Margaret Gregory was. And her 9 year old grandson, Richard, was now master. These delicate matters took time to resolve although Augusta did remain at Coole Park for the rest of her life.

Difficult years after World War One

The years following the war were horrendous for Ireland; for Augusta and her family they were terrible too. She had lost her son which was devastating enough, and six of her nephews, sons of several of her brothers, had been killed as well. More had been injured. Such was the unsung sacrifice of the families of the Big Houses of Ireland. The War of Independence, or the Black and Tan War, broke out early in 1919 and lasted for over two years. The Abbey had to close on many occasions but when there was an opportunity to run a production, Augusta Gregory was there to ensure that audiences were entertained. For extensive periods during the troubles, Augusta remained at Coole Park. On two occasions dreadful calumnies were visited upon her family. Her nephew, Frank Shaw-Taylor, was murdered by the IRA and soon afterwards her daughter-in-law, Margaret, was involved in a horrific incident. She was returning with four neighbour friends from a tennis party at a house nearby to Coole Park when they were ambushed and everyone murdered except Margaret. She never fully got over this outrage and gloom descended upon Coole Park.

When the Civil War erupted soon after the War of Independence (now brother fighting against brother and father against son), many of the ascendancy houses were burnt to the ground. Vengeance was wreaked upon the landed classes and one of the mansions destroyed was Roxborough, Augusta's childhood home. It was a sad day for the Persses, but they certainly were not alone in their grief and misery. Most of the county Galway Big Houses suffered the same fate although not so Coole Park. It was spared destruction simply because there was sufficient support amongst the locals for Lady Gregory and for what she had always done for her tenants and their families. There were a few frights which Augusta had to endure but no one ever broke in and set fire to her beloved home. For this she was, of course, mightily grateful although she grieved for her dear friends who had lost their homes regardless of whether they had been beneficent landlords or not.

In the midst of this mayhem Augusta still managed to continue writing. It acted as an antidote to the horrors which surrounded her. In these tragic years she wrote her Irish Passion play *The Story brought by Brigit*. In 1924, soon after the Free State had time to recover, this was performed at the Abbey to encouraging audiences. They seemed to appreciate the sentiment of Lady Gregory's latest work as well as being eternally grateful that Irish art had such a stalwart to lift them above the gloom of those unhappy days.

Brightness after the gloom

It was Augusta Gregory who discovered one of Ireland's true geniuses, Sean O'Casey. She encouraged him to continue to write more after having read some of his earliest contributions. To begin with Augusta's fellow directors rejected O'Casey's plays but Augusta saw in him the spark of genius. In many ways, especially in the early 1920s, it was O'Casey's play, *The Shadow of the Gunman*, which saved the Abbey from financial ruin as it appealed to the masses. It was just the play they needed in those difficult days. It made O'Casey and from then on he was a regular contributor to the works performed at the Abbey. He was, however, a shy and unworldly young man. He had been brought up as a Protestant in poverty in Dublin and it took him a considerable time to cast off this burden. His relationship with Augusta flourished and, when his powerful play *Juno and the Paycock* was produced, critics and friends alike lauded the work. In fact Augusta actually said of the play that she enjoyed it so much that she was glad that she had been born. Soon Sean was invited to Coole Park which was the ultimate accolade for Ireland's talented writers.

By 1925 it was obvious that the Abbey needed more financial help and a subsidy from the fledgling Free State government was applied for and eventually, if rather reluctantly, awarded. The amount was fairly insubstantial and there was much opposition from the directors even to accept this grant. But Augusta was hard-headed enough to realise that this money, even with the conditions attached including having to have a government director, George O'Brien, meant stability for the theatre and, more importantly, it was then able to increase the salaries to their underpaid actors and actresses. But there were always problems on the horizon. Sean O'Casey had written one of his masterpieces *The Plough and the Stars* which, when first performed, caused more riots. For a time it was touch and go whether the government subsidy would be withdrawn. They were anxious to make changes to O'Casey's play but the directors at the Abbey, driven on by Augusta, refused to let this happen. If the government were to interfere with a play and its contents now then they would surely continue to do so. They held firm and the subsidy, paltry though it was, remained. The play was an excellent one which has stood the test of time throughout the years.

When O'Casey wrote his next play, *The Silver Tassie*, Willie Yeats did not like it and said so. He had been in contact with Augusta about it and the difference of opinion came to O'Casey's ears. He was furious that such unfavourable remarks were being made about his latest work and he upped sticks and left Dublin, virtually forever. The relationship with Augusta, too, was severed, much to her disappointment and sorrow.

Augusta, by now into her 70s, remained interested and busy. She wrote her *Journals* and a number of other works which were performed at the Abbey. Her longstanding friendship with Willie Yeats changed in October 1917 when he finally married. His infatuation with Maud Gonne over the years had not resulted in her agreeing to marry him so, at the age of 52, he tied the knot with Georgie Hyde-Lees, a young woman many years his junior. In many ways Augusta felt a sense of bereavement for she had secretly hoped that there might be more than just a lasting friendship with her Willie. They remained great friends and Augusta, in due course, became a surrogate grandmother to the Yeats's two children, Anne and Michael.

In 1926 Augusta was diagnosed with breast cancer and had an operation which was successful. She had already become somewhat arthritic and a little deaf but nothing could keep her back from her various life's works – the theatre, her family and those Lane paintings. Around this time too there came a vital change at Coole Park. The house had, of course, never been Augusta's although she had always been looked upon as the mistress. During the early 1920s some of the woods had been sold and then the family decided that the house should be sold to the Forestry Commission with the proviso that she could live out her days there. This came into effect and pleased her. Margaret had not wanted the house and it seemed that Richard didn't either.

For her remaining years Augusta continued to write; she continued to invite visitors to the house and, above all, she remained totally clued in to everything around her. The end came in May 1932 with a peaceful death at Coole Park. She was buried in Galway beside one of her sisters since the family vault had been bricked up years previously. She was 80 years old and was mourned throughout the land and in many other places as well. The newspapers were full of complimentary obituaries recalling the life of this great Irishwoman. Her parting shots were the words – 'I sometimes think my life has been a series of enthusiasms' – the truth indeed.

The legacy of Augusta Gregory
In the years succeeding Augusta's death, many of her plays continued to be performed at the Abbey and in other locations throughout the country. However, the person who could have, and who should have, kept her memory more vitally alive, Willie Yeats, failed to do so. He made little reference in his remaining years (he died in 1939) to the one person who had supported and encouraged him throughout his life – Augusta Gregory. Few, if any, of her works are performed today. She has been forgotten to all intents and purposes. There are the paintings by Yeats and Mancini and the bust by Sir Jacob Epstein, but little else. There is not even a monument to their greatest daughter in Gort, Loughrea or Galway itself. Even the great Coole Park was demolished in the early 1950s leaving only a Visitor Centre and her 'Autograph' tree and the splendid walks in that lovely demesne. In my estimation, the life of this great Irishwoman is but another lost and forgotten by a nation not given to honouring its women.

Suggested reading:
1. Coxhead, Elizabeth, *Lady Gregory – a Literary Portrait*, London, 1961.
2. Gregory, Lady, *Journals 1916-1930*, London, 1946.
3. Kohfeldt, Mary Lou, *Lady Gregory – the Woman behind the Irish Renaissance*, London, 1985.
4. O'Byrne, Robert, *Hugh Lane 1875-1915*, Dublin, 2000.

Alice Milligan

Plucky Poetess

Seaton Milligan from Glencar in county Tyrone and Charlotte Burns from the county town of Omagh were married in 1862. Seaton was a practising Methodist with a keen interest in every aspect of Ireland's history. In his own childhood home and subsequently in his family home, he had a large and comprehensive library which was, in itself, quite an unusual occurrence for middle class Ulster folk.

Seaton and his wife, shortly after their marriage, went to live in Belfast where Seaton pursued his career as a commercial traveller. The first of their thirteen children was born in the city and, to begin with, life went well for the young Milligans. However sectarian riots in Belfast in those early years of the 1860s quickly impinged on their domesticity. Because they displayed a portrait of Robert Emmet (executed in Dublin in 1803) in their house, attacks were made on their property causing them to leave Belfast and return to their native county of Tyrone. It was a shock to the system but regrettably understandable.

After their return to a new house at Gortmore outside Omagh, Alice Letitia was born on 14 September 1866, the third of the Milligans' ever growing family. Soon Seaton had built another fine new house at Campsie and it was here that little Alice spent her formative years in great comfort and surrounded by a loving and educated family. She was devoted to her grandparents and particularly to a great uncle who spoke Irish. This may seem, for a Methodist man living in an Ulster county, somewhat uncharacteristic. But this was certainly not the case. The western Ulster counties of Tyrone and Londonderry were close to counties Donegal and Sligo where many of the population used Irish as their first language. Many of the young people from the west came to the regular hiring fairs held in Omagh, there to be taken on by local farmers and shopkeepers as additional help. Since they could only speak Irish the local Tyrone people had to learn the language too in order to communicate with those they had hired. And so it was that Alice took to learning Irish as well and greatly enjoyed the opportunity to do so.

The burgeoning Milligan family was relatively well off and could afford to take holidays on the north coast and in Donegal. They were greatly facilitated by making use of the new railway system which was expanding all over the island of Ireland and notably in the north west. During these early years, whilst at home and especially when she was on holiday, Alice became enthusiastic about writing poetry which was, from then on, to influence her entire life. Her father naturally enough encouraged his daughter and was proud of her first achievements. He himself was a prominent member, soon to become a Fellow, of the Royal Irish Society. This organisation had been founded in 1849 with the express interest in preserving and showing to best advantage the plethora of ancient Irish monuments in every corner of the country. Seaton involved himself totally in the society and even arranged various outings for members to visit the local antiquities in their home area. Alice herself often joined her father on these trips which further cemented her interest in Ireland's history.

Alice was close to her father and even assisted him in publishing an early form of a tourist guide in 1888. As a Victorian father, Seaton was unique. He treated all his children as adults and shared all his knowledge with them. In addition he treated his daughters as equal to his sons. The parents and the children were devoted to one another although they did suffer the tragic loss of two of their sons by 1875. The Milligans were a highly respected family in the area and pillars of the society in which they lived.

Another move to Belfast
In 1878 Seaton was appointed a director of his prestigious firm with its headquarters in the Bank Buildings in central Belfast. This meant, of course, another move to the city and there they occupied a large Victorian terrace house at 1 Royal Terrace at the bottom of the Lisburn Road. Here the socially conscious Alice, now 12 years old, appreciated how the two halves of society lived. There were her wealthy neighbours in their grand houses alongside hers but opposite there were the poor and destitute of the city living in the great workhouse situated exactly opposite their Royal Terrace home. The needs of the less fortunate in the population were to affect and influence Alice's life from that point onwards.

Alice became a pupil at the prestigious Methodist College where she turned out to be an able student winning a number of prizes along the scholastic way. However she was not exactly a model pupil regularly receiving reprimands from her teachers, particularly her Classics master. This teacher had also taught CS Parnell who, as it so happened, often required chastisement for various misdemeanours. Throughout her senior school career, Alice often wondered why some attempt had not been made by the educational hierarchy to include the learning of the Irish language into the curriculum. Perhaps this, even then, was a step too far from a college chiefly populated by Protestant children, although such a subject would certainly have been appreciated by Miss Alice Milligan.

Seaton was prospering in his new post in the city centre and soon considered it necessary for his large family to purchase a seaside house to escape the rigours of the city. A house was bought on the county Down coast at Donaghadee and a significant part of the year, from Easter to the end of October, was spent there. Once again the railway proved useful in conveying father and his children to work and school in Belfast.

Early adulthood and immersion in Irish nationalism
In 1886, not long before her 20th birthday, Alice set out for King's College, London to study English. She only remained there for one academic year before returning to take up a position as a governess at the Ladies' Collegiate College in Londonderry. It seems certain that she had not qualified as a teacher although she seemed happy to be appointed to this particular post. There she made friends with a talented young Scottish music teacher, Marjorie Arthur. Alice and Marjorie became bosom

companions although Alice herself had no leanings to pursue music as a career which obviously meant a great deal to Marjorie and which also constituted a large part of the lives of a number of her sisters. One of them, Charlotte, became an accomplished musician who had helped to found the Irish Folksong Society which became a moving force in the music scene throughout the British Isles in those latter years of the 19th century.

In 1888 Alice, still intrigued and enthralled by the Irish language, headed for Dublin. It should be remembered that these latter years of the 1800s were probably the most stimulating period in Ireland's fight to attain its real Irish identity. On her arrival in Dublin Alice immediately gravitated towards the Irish Academy, where she studied, and the National Library, where she immersed herself in mixing with other students with similar views to her own. Although always a keen advocate of the Irish language, Alice had to admit to being a poor learner. She had the good fortune to meet Michael Davitt, one of the founders of the Land League and of many other Irish Ireland organisations, who encouraged Alice to persevere in the learning of Irish.

The name on everyone's lips in Dublin at the time was that of Charles Stewart Parnell. By the mid 1880s he was undoubtedly the 'Uncrowned King of Ireland'. He could do nothing wrong and whatever he touched turned to gold. But, by 1891, his life had been turned upside down following the revelation of his affair with the wife of an MP colleague of his, Katherine O'Shea. He had by now wholly fallen from grace and Alice endured the sad experience of hearing her beloved Parnell speak for about his last time in Ireland in June 1891 at Inchicore. He looked crestfallen and dejected and was evidently a very sick man. He was soon to marry his dearest Katie and then to die in that October at the tragically early age of 45. Alice, who had always held Parnell in high esteem, was heartbroken and even went so far as to lay the blame for his death on the Roman Catholic church. She decided there and then to leave Dublin and return to the north to her parental home.

Poetry and writing

Seaton and his wife had, by the time of Alice's return from Dublin, taken another comfortable summer house in Bangor, county Down. Alice quickly settled there and enjoyed the company of her many friends at this new location. However, by this stage in her life aged 25, it seemed more and more unlikely that she would ever marry. Her nationalist views were popular with her close friends but were rather frowned upon by many members of her family and by those young men who might have sought her hand in marriage. Alice was considered self-opinionated and her politics did not fit in well with prospective suitors. But this situation never fazed Alice and by now she was writing some of her best poetry. Tragedy struck in February 1892 when her dear friend, Marjorie Arthur, died while still a very young woman. Alice dedicated a poem to her called *If this could be*, the final lines of which summed up how much Alice was going to miss Marjorie.

Just to be near you – just to hear your voice,

We two together and no other near (though others too are dear)

Nor would I miss the mountains and the sea

If you could come to me.

Life in Bangor was an ever-changing one with a number of her brothers and sisters marrying and others now away from home. She was beginning to feel slightly hemmed in and she became somewhat depressed. She was fortunate, however, to be able to resolve the situation herself as she began to realise how talented she was in the field of writing. She completed her first novel, *A Royal Democrat*, by the end of 1892. Her energies were concentrated on Irish literature which coincided with the formation in 1893, by Douglas Hyde, of the Gaelic League. The Irish arts, crafts, literature and sport were now in the ascendancy and, as far as Alice was concerned, this was the time for nationalism and Irishness to flourish.

The Irish literary movement

Seaton made a further shrewd move when he sold his Royal Terrace house and moved to the Cave Hill area of Belfast. Here much of Alice's true interest in nationalist politics and literature was cemented. She met the poetess Ethna Carbery (whose real name was Anna Johnston) and the Quaker firebrand, Bulmer Hobson. By now Alice was meeting many of the prominent men and women in the Irish movements both at her home, where Seaton was pleased to welcome them, and also in the homes of her friends. FJ Biggar, who was an influential and well-connected Belfast man, became a great friend and introduced Alice and Ethna to none other than Roger Casement who happened to be visiting Biggar at his home.

Alice and Ethna visited Dublin again in 1893 where they met yet more highflying personalities like WB Yeats and the county Armagh poet and nationalist, AE (George Russell). Alice was certainly moving in the right circles and her poetry was attracting a great deal of attention. She was gaining a reputation as a poet of note. At this time her friendship with Yeats was flourishing. He had heard of Alice's work from his own friends and decided to cultivate the bond. As was Yeats's wont, and realising that Alice was very likely to become a rival in the field of poetry, he encouraged her to write more prose. Alice, however, clearly understood what Yeats was up to and made up her own mind as to what she wanted to write and the direction she wanted to pursue. They remained wary friends throughout their lives until Yeats's death in 1939. But it was clear to see that Alice Milligan had come of age. She continued to visit Dublin as often as possible, once more using the railway network. For a while she reworked a few of her novels into plays but these were less successful than her favoured poetry. She even took to using a pseudonym 'Iris Olkyrn' when writing but no one could see any reason for her doing so. She herself also seemed uncertain as to why she used it – perhaps it was nothing more than a mere deflection. Maybe Yeats had got to her.

From 1893 Alice's reputation was further enhanced. Those who reviewed Irish writing and poetry in the newspapers predictably mentioned Alice's name. She was now a celebrated poetess and one whose writing was worthy of praise. Her poetry was vigorous and strong and, whilst she lauded Ireland's past, she was always keenest on stories from the north of Ireland, the land of her birth. It might be said that her religion was Ireland and her writings became the embodiment of her patriotism.

Now approaching her 30th birthday, Alice took centre stage in northern nationalism. She became president of the Belfast branch of the Irish Women's Association in 1895; she was a founder of the Belfast Gaelic League; she helped found the Henry Joy McCracken Literary Society and became one of its vice presidents. The Society's principal aim was to teach children something of their country's history. And it is pleasing to note that these various societies accepted membership from women as well as from men. This was quite unlike many of the clubs and literary organisations in Dublin where women like Maud Gonne and Constance Markievicz had to set up women's clubs since the men folk would not permit female membership.

Then Alice took yet another momentous step, this time into newspaper publishing.

The Northern Patriot and *Shan van Vocht*

The McCracken Literary Society proved extremely popular and soon a reading room and its own library were set up. This was uncommon in Belfast and both these facilities attracted many visitors, not just children but adults as well. They also published a newspaper called *The Northern Patriot*. As enthusiastic as ever Alice and Ethna set about encouraging contributions for the publication and immediately became sub editors. Considering that they only lasted in their editorial positions for just three editions, the fact that they actually met Maud Gonne in Belfast and elicited from her an article on the Amnesty campaign seeking the release of the so-called 'dynamiters' (who included Tom Clarke – a signatory of the proclamation at the Easter Rising) was nothing less than remarkable. Why they only lasted for three issues, and were probably sacked, is unknown but a possible explanation is that Alice was still an ardent pro-Parnellite and this reason alone could well have led to her dismissal. Ethna would presumably have resigned, or got sacked too, because of her friendship with Alice.

But these two young women were not to be easily put off, especially by mere men. Without further ado, they set up their own rival newspaper which they called *Shan van Vocht*, which is roughly translated as *The Poor Old Woman*.

The paper was an instant success and it was not long before they had pushed *The Northern Patriot* off the streets. They worked exceedingly hard to keep their paper going. They sought contributors from all parts of Ireland; they inveigled people of prominence to write articles for them; they revived Irish nationalism through the pages of the publication; and they even wrote and stamped the envelopes themselves before going to the post office to send them out. They were also forward thinking and decided early on to appoint an agent in the United States. The Irish American lobby was an important audience at this time. Their newspaper filled another gap which enabled the Irish diaspora to express their views in a paper which circulated, though with difficulty, throughout Ireland itself. Amongst its early contributors were Arthur Griffith, who some years later was to found Sinn Fein, and the founder of the Gaelic League, Douglas Hyde, who would go on to become the first president of Ireland in 1938. He wrote many of his articles in Irish too. James Connolly, the Scottish born trade unionist and socialist, who would go on to lay down his life for Ireland after the Easter Rising in 1916, also wrote for *Shan* although his pieces often struck the wrong chords with Alice and Ethna.

In the end and after three very busy years at the helm of *Shan van Vocht*, Alice and Ethna bravely took the decision to close down what had been an immensely popular paper in favour of Arthur Griffith's weekly publication *The United Irishman*. Griffith and his young and brilliant protégé, Willie Rooney, (who was sadly to die just a year or two later), now had an all-Ireland cause worth supporting. This was to lead to the emergence of the Sinn Fein organisation of 1905 and the erstwhile editors of *Shan van Vocht* were happy to join forces with their Dublin colleagues. The years spent on their newspaper had been a rewarding period for Alice Milligan. She saw the true worth of uniting every form of opinion in Ireland's struggle for constitutional independence and her contribution had been freely acknowledged and appreciated. Indeed it was Maud Gonne who declared of their excellent writing that Dublin would have to look to its laurels if it were not to be outdone by the perceptive journalism emanating from Belfast.

Alice Milligan's life was full. She was spending every hour of the day writing, editing and undertaking many lecture engagements. She was a sought-after speaker to all sorts of groups in Belfast and beyond. She was happy to go wherever she was invited and enjoyed setting up various clubs and reading rooms. But, on the negative side, she had become rather bossy and hard to work with. She loved to lay down rules and woe betide anyone who countered them. But the small and aggressive Alice and the dreamy-eyed and tender Ethna made a formidable pair who worked well together.

Towards the turn of the century
The year 1898 was a significant one in the life of a country where anniversaries were important. This was the centenary year of the bloody and abortive United Irishmen's rising mainly in counties Wexford and Wicklow in 1798. Alice was

appointed as the organising secretary for Ulster (where there had been two smaller risings in counties Down and Antrim) and, as ever, she took her responsibilities very seriously. She was a devotee of Theobald Wolfe Tone, the leader of the United Irishmen (who actually had not even been in Ireland during those horrific months of the summer of 1798). She wrote a little book *The Life of Theobald Wolfe Tone* which she published in 1898 through the offices of *Shan*. Along with Ethna she travelled by train throughout county Donegal and lectured on the United Irishmen in most of the towns of that wild and beautiful county to large and appreciative audiences. The names of Alice Milligan, Ethna Carbery and Ethna's friend and soon to be fiancé, Seumas MacManus, were on the lips of everyone. The local newspapers were full of reports of the enthusiasm of these young women from the north.

Alice was always conscious of her difficulty in mastering the Irish language. She realised, much to her chagrin, that she was not cut out to be a fluent Irish speaker and no matter what she seemed to do, she never became proficient. But, by way of proving herself, she did attempt to write some plays in Irish and before the 20th century dawned one of Alice's plays was accepted by Willie Yeats and Lady Gregory to be performed in the Abbey theatre. This was entitled *The Last Feast of Fianna* and she was delighted to see how well the critical Dublin newspapers and the knowledgeable city audiences had received it.

In 1902, just as her friendship with Ethna Carbery was becoming all the more important to her, tragedy struck. Ethna had, in the late summer of 1901, married her dear Seumas MacManus from her beloved Donegal and had gone to live there. But now, just 8 months after her marriage, Ethna took ill and died on 2 April 1902. Alice was heartbroken at having lost such a companion and she felt even more saddened for poor Seumas. In her poem *The House of the Apple Trees* Alice poignantly describes Ethna's little home which she was only to live in for such a short time.

> *I know it will be beautiful in May*
> *But – she has gone away*

Two more calamities severely affected Alice around these early years of the 20th century. In 1901 the brilliant young poet and writer, Willie Rooney, died in Dublin aged only 29. Alice could only ponder at how much Ireland had lost at the premature passing of her friend. In 1903, just a year after Ethna's death, Alice's sister, Evelyn, committed suicide by walking out into the sea at Bangor. This horror was further confounded by the fact that their youngest brother, Charles, had witnessed the tragic event as he stood helpless on the shore.

New horizons and family responsibilities

Having mourned for those who had recently died so tragically, Alice now looked forward with her former enthusiasm. By this time the Gaelic League and all its various events had taken hold throughout the entire country. A popular activity in those days was lantern lecturing. Alice was invited to travel the country presenting these talks and she greatly enjoyed these undertakings. In 1904 she headed off for far-flung Cork where she immersed herself in Gaelic League activities which, apart from her inspired lecturing, also included setting up language and Irish dancing classes. At the same time she collected much-needed funds for the League. And no sooner had she completed her arduous tasks in Cork than she was whisked away to the other end of the country to county Londonderry where she repeated everything she had done in Cork and with every bit as much vigour and passion. Yet despite all this hard work and tiresome travelling Alice still found time to write. She was by now 40 years old and at this time had formed a close literary relationship with George Russell, known as AE, her fellow northerner poet from county Armagh. This first decade of the new century was a productive one for Alice in every aspect of her interests. She continued to write inspired poetry; she spent time mixing with her literary friends and she looked forward with much anticipation to what was next in store for her in every field of the arts.

Family life, however, now encroached upon Alice's career. As an unmarried daughter and with so many of her large number of brothers and sisters leaving home to get married, the responsibility of caring for her aging parents in Bangor devolved upon her. She was expected to remain at home regardless of her increasing fame as an Irish poet of great note. But she took on these duties as a faithful daughter whilst doing her best to keep abreast of what was happening in the Irish literary scene. Needless to say, however, many of her Gaelic League and other connections had to take a back seat and, of necessity, she had to work and make preparations for forthcoming events at home on the county Down coast. There were, thankfully, silver linings within these clouds of constraint. Her brother, William, was a fairly talented writer himself and both he and Alice cooperated in the writing and publishing of a great novel about the founding of Dublin. To undertake so much research for such an academic tome must have taken the pair of them much time and heartache to prepare, but they succeeded to much acclaim.

Another up and coming poet, Thomas McDonagh, who taught at Patrick Pearse's St Enda's school in Dublin, became a friend and correspondent of Alice's. He was highly impressed by her poetry and went so far as to say that Alice 'was the most Irish of living poets and even better than the revered Thomas Davis'. This was praise indeed for to be compared to Davis was indeed a worthy acclamation. By now, around 1914, Alice was at the zenith of her career. She was now almost 50 years old.

1916 – a seismic year for Alice and for Ireland

Alice's personal life was utterly shattered in this year of 1916. Her mother, for whom Alice had been caring, died in January and was buried in county Tyrone outside Omagh. Alice then had to travel to London to care for her sister, Charlotte, who also soon died in March. Then her father, unable to bear the strain of his wife's and his daughter's deaths, succumbed in April. Within three short months Alice had lost a large and significant part of her loving family. Then, as it were to foist tragedy upon calamity, the Easter Rising broke out in Dublin at the end of April and Alice was devastated to discover that her dear friend, Thomas McDonagh, had been executed for his part in the uprising. He had been one of the seven signatories to the proclamation of an Irish Republic delivered by Patrick Pearse outside the General Post Office on Monday 24 April.

Somehow or other Alice managed to get on with her life by immediately showing an interest in those who had been imprisoned after the Rising and visiting many of them in prison. In August Alice sat daily in the London courtroom where her friend, Roger Casement, was on trial for his life. She was outside the prison when he was hanged at Pentonville on 3 August 1916. Her unsuccessful campaign to secure the release of Casement seemed to crown a horrific and terrible year for Alice Milligan. For the remainder of the year she stayed in England regularly continuing her prison visiting including making trips to the Frongoch internment camp in north Wales where many of those involved in the Easter Rising, as well as many who were not, were incarcerated, including Michael Collins who was in custody there for the duration.

Life moves on and responsibilities become greater

Alice returned to Ireland in 1917 but two years later, without any regular income, she was obliged to go to live with her brother, Ernest and his family, near Bath. Her brother, William, was also there. By 1920 Alice and William had come back to Dublin but, because of William's connections with the British Army, they had to flee north to Belfast. By now the Irish Civil War had broken out bringing untold misery to many families throughout the island. Alice abhorred this war of father against son and brother against brother. Like so many other like-minded and influential people, she condemned the utter futility of the conflict. Alice countered her rage at the war by writing perhaps her best ever poetry and her poem *Till Ferdia Came* epitomised her anguish. Soon the toing and froing between Ireland and England resumed when she went back with William to Ernest's home. This time Alice had, at least, a goal in mind. She acted as governess to Ernest's three daughters. She felt as if she was now of use and not just a burden on her brother. With the death of yet another sister, Edith, the Milligans were fast diminishing.

By 1932 Alice had come back to Ireland for good. William and Alice went to live in Mountfield, county Tyrone, which was then a staunchly republican area. William was proving to be troublesome yet he was still able to do some writing and, with the help of their friend, Bulmer Hobson, he and Alice produced another book *The Dynamite Drummer*. Unfortunately sales did not go well which rather depressed Alice. In the household by now were William's wife and son. Most of the domestic responsibilities fell upon Alice who found her sister-in-law hard to live with. William died in 1937 having been predeceased by his son who died following a stroke at the early age of 26. Alice had then to care for William's widow which proved a thankless task. At length she too died leaving Alice on her own.

The eccentric Miss Milligan became an object of pity around Mountfield. Her remaining brothers realised the desperate situation as far as Alice's finances, or rather the lack of them, were concerned and immediately saw to it that their sister's bills were paid. When the artistic and literary world realised the dire straits that their friend had found herself in, they immediately set about making a collection for her. This generous gesture netted a much-needed sum of over £270. Living in such austere conditions in this little village were not conducive to Alice writing much more. She had few if any contacts now with her former colleagues and there was little of academic interest in Mountfield. It was a far cry from the glittering lights of Dublin and even Belfast. The sight of the once eminent Irish poetess wandering down to the village shop followed by her army of cats must have been a sobering spectacle.

Out of the blue, however, in 1941 the National University of Ireland conferred an honorary degree upon Alice which pleased her enormously. At least those academic luminaries in Dublin had not entirely forgotten Alice. Becoming Dr Alice Milligan was at least recognition of her work although it brought her no financial reward. She was still as poor as a church mouse. However one positive step was taken after the conferring of the degree. Subscriptions were sought and collected and consideration was finally given to having a compilation of her poetry written. In 1950 some of her poems, along with a number of Ethna Carbery's and Seumas MacManus' were put into print as *We Sang for Ireland*. Yet again, however, very little money accrued to Alice following this publication. She was destined never to reap any financial benefit from her wonderful poetry.

By 1951, when Alice was 85, she moved to the townland of Tyrcur, five miles north of Omagh, where she was taken in by a kindly widow, Mrs McSwiggan, and her two daughters. This proved a very happy arrangement and at last Alice was able to spend her final days in comfort. On 13 April 1953 she died peacefully in her sleep. She was buried at the little graveyard at Drumragh with only a small number of mourners present to record her passing. Yet another of Ireland's fine and honoured women had passed away without the world in general and Ireland in particular ever even noticing. As the years passed by very little of Alice Milligan's works were committed to print. The year after her passing, 1954, Henry Mangan edited a book of 61 of Alice's poems, entitled simply *Poems*. This surely is shameful and only a half-hearted attempt to commemorate a woman of such renown. A unique individual, an Irish patriot and a revered poetess had passed away without the country even acknowledging the fact. Perhaps now is the time for a further volume of Alice Milligan's poems to be published. It would give today's generations the opportunity to savour the best of Irish poetry.

Suggested reading
1. Johnston, Sheila Turner, *Alice – a Life of Alice Milligan*, Omagh, 1994.
2. Johnston, Sheila Turner (ed), *The Harper of the Only God – a Selection of Poems by Alice Milligan*, Omagh, 1993.

Maud Gonne

Reckless Romantic

The story of Maud Gonne is known, at least in some measure, to most people interested in Ireland's history. Born in England on 21 December 1866, Edith Maud Gonne went on to become a revered figure in this island's recent past. She was the elder of two daughters born to a wealthy couple, Edith and Thomas Gonne, in Tongham in Surrey at a time of relative quiet in the land of her birth but at a time of great upheaval in the land of her adoption. Ireland was still suffering from the devastation caused by the Great Famine and was soon to be affected by yet another abortive rising when the Fenian rebellion of 1867 came and went in the blink of an eye.

Maud's sister, Kathleen, was born two years later. Their father, who was in the army, was posted in 1868 to the Curragh, the largest camp for the Crown forces in Ireland. He spent a great deal of time away from his family such was the demand for soldiers to keep the peace throughout the vast British Empire. Then, in 1871, tragedy struck the family when Edith Gonne succumbed to TB and died leaving her little daughters, just 2 and 4 years old, and her husband stricken with grief. It was fortunate that the children had a nanny who was able to take over their care when their father had to leave home for yet another posting far from home. Since he was still at the Curragh at the time of his wife's death, Thomas Gonne moved the family to Howth, that idyllic coastal village north of Dublin. Here the girls settled well and found great pleasure in mixing with the children of local families there on the hill of Howth. One thing quickly struck the sensitive Maud. The youngsters near their new home were not nearly as privileged as those they had known, albeit briefly, in affluent Surrey. They were poor and, although by no means destitute, yet somehow in need of extra love and care. This was given to them by the little Miss Gonne. She may only have been a child herself but she seemed to be able to help them in their trying home circumstances.

Maud had learnt her first lesson in life – there was a real difference between children of rich and poor backgrounds. Even at just 5 years of age Maud was conscious that life for these Irish children was much less privileged than hers. It was to become a lesson which, throughout her long life, she would never forget.

But Maud and Kathleen had little time to settle in their newly discovered Irish surroundings. Their father considered that it would be better for his daughters' education that they should leave Ireland and return to England. For the following ten years they were moved from pillar to post amongst many of their relatives there. Aged 8 and 6 the girls were first sent to live with their great aunt Augusta in London; this placement was not a success. They were summarily removed. They were then landed with a brother of their late mother, their uncle Frank, who lived in Richmond. These may have been sumptuous surroundings, but it turned out to be another unhappy home. There was, however, one positive in this house, their lovely and kind aunt Emily, a Portuguese lady, who loved the girls although she herself suffered at the hands of her browbeating husband.

All the while their father, Thomas, was enduring army postings in such exotic places as Vienna, Bosnia, India and even in the snowy wastes of St Petersburg. It is hard to imagine his heart-searching at being continually separated from his daughters. But at least he was able to have the girls with him sometimes especially when they went to live in the south of France where they had gone to help Maud recover from bouts of ill health. This was family life which Maud and Kathleen had so rarely known. They took to the chance of being with their father with great gusto. As they got older, they were given the chance to act as their father's hostesses when he had company at their home. It was even said that Maud was often taken as her father's companion, something which pleased her greatly as she and her father were very close.

By 1883, Maud now being over 16 years old, the Gonnes returned to Ireland. Maud quickly found herself involved with her neighbours in caring for their needs. She would have been seen as the privileged young woman next door, yet she was considered to be a young woman keen to help. Her friends would have been curious, but probably quite proud, to hear that their friend Maud was to be presented to Queen Victoria as a debutante. They could scarcely comprehend what being 'presented' meant, but they were anxious to hear from Maud herself, on her return from London, what precisely had happened that day.

As so often happened in the lives of the great and the good as well as in the homes of the poor and underprivileged, tragedy was to strike the Gonne family yet again. On 3 November 1886, Thomas Gonne died of typhoid aged just 51. His wealth and position in life had not saved him from a scourge which regularly affected the people in Ireland and beyond. Maud was barely 20 and Kathleen just two years younger and their lives had hit another low.

Although they were by now young adults, the Gonne sisters were obliged to return to London to live with yet another uncle, Thomas's elder brother, William. He was not easy to get on with and the girls soon grew to greatly dislike him.

As they were coming to terms with the rules and regulations of uncle William's strict household, yet another bombshell was dropped. They were introduced to a young woman called Margaret Wilson who had just recently borne Thomas Gonne's illegitimate child, a little daughter, Eileen. William rather assumed that Maud would show disdain and would turn away from the unfortunate pair. But this was not the case as far as Maud and Kathleen were concerned. Uncle William had not reckoned with Maud's social conscience. She made sure, from that day forth, that Margaret and her child would be looked after and would want for nothing. Consequently their stay with their uncle William came to an abrupt halt and they moved, once more, to the home of yet another Gonne uncle, Charlie. He had two delightful daughters himself, Chotie and May, and Maud and her sister became great and lasting companions and friends to these young women.

The life of Maud Gonne, therefore, had already taken so many twists and turns that it would not have been remarkable if she had turned her face against the world. This was not in Maud's nature and she was all the more determined to find her feet – and to do so quickly. Her mean spirited uncle William had another surprise in store. He informed the girls that their father had not left them much of an inheritance. This seemed strange as it always appeared that he had been a man of some independent means. It soon transpired, however, that Thomas had, in fact, left them comfortably off allowing Maud and Kathleen to move on in the knowledge that there were funds available to assist them in the future lives.

Thus the young years of the life of Maud Gonne had come and gone. She had suffered many grievous losses and had endured many family vicissitudes. Notwithstanding she had discovered a number of personal qualities, such as her love and care for the needy and her worthy social conscience that would stand her in good stead throughout her life.

Life was then to take a different and more secretive turn. Now aged 21 Maud returned to the south of France, to Royat. Her health was still a concern and she found the climate on the shores of the Mediterranean much to her liking. Fate now intervened in two guises, both personal and political. She met a Frenchman called Lucien Millevoye who literally swept Maud off her feet. They became lovers and, at the same time, political soul mates. Millevoye encouraged Maud to fight for the freedom of Ireland, her adopted homeland. He himself was fighting for the freedom of his own homeland, Alsace Lorraine. They entered into an alliance whereby they would each concentrate on their own respective parts of Europe. It was not long before Millevoye had coined a phrase that would stick to Maud throughout her life. She would become Ireland's 'Joan of Arc'.

Maud soon found herself involved in political intrigue and, at Millevoye's insistence, she travelled illegally to Russia to deliver secret papers. It is of little importance what these documents were, but it does open another chapter in the life of this feisty and thrill-seeking young woman. She had taken up the torch on behalf of Ireland; she had taken a decision to expend her considerable energies to seek independence for Ireland; she had taken a defining step on the road which would undoubtedly lead to confrontation and opposition. She appeared assured in the knowledge that there would be troubles in store for her in the future and she appeared to relish the prospect. She had made her bed; she would now have to lie in it.

The Irish personalities
Having experienced the adrenalin rush of her illegal entry into, and her speedy flight from, mother Russia, Maud made her way to London to further the cause espoused by Millevoye. There she made it her business to contact and meet Michael Davitt, the one-armed Irish MP and leader of the Land League in recent years. She fully understood the work and energy that Davitt had put into his campaign to return land to the impoverished Irish from the clutches of the Anglo Irish landlords. She knew he had met with considerable success and she wanted to

learn from him what she might do to further his mission. Davitt rebuffed Maud's keen advances and informed her that he was not interested in her idealistic plans to undertake her own form of good works. In all likelihood he was suspicious of this Englishwoman and her romantic approaches to the needs of the suffering Irish. How wrong he was, but it would take him years to acknowledge his mistake.

Maud was not to be put off and, on meeting another of the Irish MPs, Tim Harrington, she soon found herself in the wilds of county Donegal in the far north west of Ireland. There she threw herself into helping many evicted tenants, thrown on the roadside by many cruel and vindictive landlords. She assisted in the building of Land League huts, accommodation provided through public donations to provide homes for the needy and dispossessed. She made an immediate impression on those she worked with and with the unfortunates she was helping. Few would ever forget the way in which Miss Gonne had thrown herself selflessly into the work to which she was so obviously committed. The first practical steps had now been taken by Maud on the path which was to make her a household name in Irish homes for generations.

In 1889, when she was 22, Maud was to meet someone who would dog her life for the next 30 years – William Butler Yeats. His name was to become almost synonymous with that of Maud Gonne – mention one name, either Yeats's or Maud's, and the other name would immediately be spoken. Yeats and Maud were truly intermingled in respect not only of their own private lives but also with the life of Ireland until well into the 20th century. At the same time in Dublin, Maud was soon to make the acquaintance of more prominent Irishmen. One was John O'Leary, an old Republican who had spent 20 years in jail and in exile from Ireland. He had a lifelong effect on Maud for he was able to describe to her what life was like for someone like himself who had suffered for Ireland yet had been happy to do so. She struck up a friendship with Arthur Griffith and his friend Willie Rooney. Both men were in the forefront of pushing for independence for their country but by purely constitutional methods. They ran the Celtic Literary Society to which were invited the best known thinkers and debaters of the day. Maud hastened to join this august company to listen to the views of those whose words and thoughts counted in Dublin at the time. But she had not reckoned with male dominated prejudice. She was not permitted to enter the premises to hear what their members had to say. They were all men and women were not welcome. This Maud found abhorrent and she took careful note of the attitudes of the men. Later she would make her own contribution to current thinking in the city. Women would speak and would not be gagged by the narrow-mindedness of men.

A return to France
Maud Gonne spent yet more time back in France. Millevoye still held an amount of control over her and, on 11 January 1890, an event occurred which was to colour her entire life. A son was born to Maud and her lover. He was named Georges but

very few people knew of his existence. Her family did not know; Yeats did not know; her friends in Ireland did not know. The secret affair amazingly was kept under wraps for many years to come. How she managed to keep her secret from the public and her friends remains to this day a complete mystery.

But she was soon back in Ireland, back to her work in county Donegal. Her son was simply left with his nanny in France. In Ireland she was persona non grata. Yet another of her Irish MP acquaintances, Pat O'Brien, informed Maud that there was a warrant out for her arrest. It was more and more obvious that Maud Gonne was becoming, not only a modern day heroine to the needy in Donegal, but also a threat to the British establishment. She had made her mark in double quick time – in a good way and equally in a bad way. She left Donegal in great haste and returned to France. She probably, on reflection, understood that she had established her credentials in her endeavours to fight for Ireland's rights even quicker than she could ever have imagined. Outwardly she was pleased; inwardly she was gloating for she then realised that Maud Gonne was now a name to be reckoned with, a name to be, if not feared by the British, then at least one highlighted on their lists of suspects and unwelcome visitors.

However 1891 was to prove to be a gloomy year for Maud Gonne. Her relationship with Lucien Millevoye was foundering and her sister's marriage was proving unsatisfactory and unhappy. And then, to crown this miserable year, little Georges, then just 19 months old, died of meningitis on 31 August. This was a great blow to his parents which had the effect of Lucien and Maud reconciling to some degree. Sadly too was the fact that very few people knew of the child's existence and therefore there was not the usual sharing of condolence with family members and close friends. Typically, and without further ado, Maud threw herself into her work for her causes and commenced a lecture tour of France propounding her views on Irish freedom and on other worthy causes – at least worthy in her own eyes. She was an instant success and everyone seemed to want to hear Maud Gonne and to read about her in the newspapers. She was becoming a real personality and revered by an adoring public.

She now set her sights, by adding her not inconsiderable voice, on the plight of those known as treason felony prisoners. These were Irishmen who had been captured on various dynamite raids in England on behalf of the Irish cause and had been imprisoned for many years. One such man was Tom Clarke who was to become revered in Ireland's history in later years as one of the signatories to the Easter Rising in 1916 and who was executed. Maud was able, by her grit and tenacity, to obtain the release of a number of these prisoners and this added to her growing fame. She simply could not refuse the call of any organisation or person to assist in improving their conditions or their lot in life. There is little wonder that she continued to be a thorn in the flesh of the British authorities.

So she returned to France to escape the clutches of the powers that be at Dublin Castle. She remained there almost constantly for the next 4 years, from 1893 until 1897. She went back to Millevoye who felt truly vindicated that Maud had followed his advice and taken up the cudgels to further the cause of a free Ireland. She went off on more lecture tours throughout France, which were much praised by Millevoye and, naturally enough, by the French press which continued to cover Maud's lectures assiduously. Her star continued in the ascendant.

On 6 August 1894, Maud gave birth to a second child, a daughter called Iseult. The relationship with Millevoye was evidently still flourishing. Yet Maud's friendship with Willie Yeats carried on. He still did not know of the existence of her children, the lost little Georges and now the arrival of Iseult. This seems almost incredible since Yeats considered himself the very soul mate of Maud. How she kept her secret is hard to comprehend. Perhaps he did know although he certainly never talked about his suspicions to Maud.

With her faithful nanny caring for her daughter, Maud set about editing a newspaper which she called *L'Irlande Libre*. Not only had she the responsibility of editing the paper she also had to ensure that there were articles to fill it. She wrote much herself and Millevoye, and probably Yeats, contributed to its pages. It was a formidable task to perform but she continued with the paper for a number of years. It was during this time that Millevoye and Maud finally drifted apart.

Ireland and America

Maud felt drawn yet again to Ireland. There were the protests against Queen Victoria's visit to Dublin for her diamond jubilee celebrations to be arranged and with her usual gusto Maud, who had, of course, previously been presented to the queen, entered into the spirit of objection and non-compliance. There would be alternatives for the ordinary population to counter the parties being run in connection with the royal visit. These republican festivities were a success with more children enjoying these parties than those organised by the loyal citizens of the capital. She also found herself becoming involved with committees which were preparing for the so-called '98 celebrations to commemorate the 1798 rebellion which had resulted in the deaths of 30,000 Irishmen and women in Ireland's bloodiest conflict ever. Maud was in demand which was, in many ways, surprising in that she was not even a permanent resident of the country. It does clearly indicate, however, the esteem in which she was held by many people.

During these frenetic meetings and arrangements, Maud met James Connolly, that firebrand Scot whose speeches on behalf of the downtrodden trade unionists and socialists were becoming legendary. They got on very well which says a lot for the perceptions of Connolly who clearly appreciated what the likes of Maud Gonne and Constance Markievicz were doing and saying in the cause of the poor and needy who were also central to Connolly's own thinking. Maud always had an admiration for what Connolly was doing and she was able to give him practical help when, for example, she paid a fine to get him released from a short spell in prison in 1897.

Maud then made her first trip to America where she undertook an exhausting tour of many of that great country's major cities. It is easy for us today, in an age of speedy travel to all parts of the world, to forget how strenuous such a visit and subsequent tour would have been. There would have been a lengthy sea voyage followed by stressful train journeys throughout that vast country. But Maud survived the trip and made a wonderful success of it. She was in great demand with people flocking in droves to hear her speak about the hopes and expectations for freeing Ireland from the British yoke. There were also a number of more delicate appointments to keep in America. There were, and have continued to be, differences and squabbles amongst the various Irish American groups. Maud did her best to resolve as many disputes as she could although she had to admit, as many others had done in the past, that it would take the patience and resolve of Solomon to bring all these disparate groups together.

On her return to Ireland she reported on her successes and disappointments before travelling to county Mayo to assist those in that impoverished county suffering from the effects of another near famine. Her tenacity once more paid off for she was able, presumably with assistance from others working there as well, to gain help and concessions for the people to improve their lot. It has been said that Maud was hero-worshipped in Mayo following her intervention on behalf of the local people. She had only spent a relatively short time there and yet the differences and improvements she had made must have been significant. The Irish were not given to hero-worship unless the circumstances warranted it and Maud evidently had made the grade. English born, Maud Gonne was quickly becoming a model Irishwoman.

Life becomes more complicated

At length in 1898 Maud felt that it was time to confide in her closest friends the secrets of her mysterious past. Her relationship with Lucien Millevoye had come to an end and she was finding life impossible to bear. On one of Willie Yeats's frequent visits to her in Paris, she decided to tell him the story about her long association with Millevoye and, more dramatically, that she had borne him two children. By now Iseult was 4 years old and little Georges had been dead for over 7 years. It was an emotionally draining time for both of them for, apart from Millevoye, Yeats was closest to Maud. Whether or not the revelations came as a complete surprise to Yeats is not known but one might suspect that he had known something of what had been going on. Now he knew and presumably he thought that the time had come for Maud to accept his proposal of marriage. But the time was not yet ripe, nor was it ever to be if he had only but known. Needless to say Maud remained Yeats's dearest confidante.

By 1899, with Britain at war in South Africa against the Boers, Maud visited London to join the campaign to dissuade Irishmen from fighting for the British. In those days, more than 30% of all British soldiers were Irishmen drawn from every part of the island. One of those influential men in Dublin to participate in this movement was Arthur Griffith whom Maud had previously met. He encouraged Maud to write articles on the subject for his nationalist newspaper *United Irishman*. This she was happy to do and, as ever, her prolific pieces on the issue were pertinent and found favour with the readers. Griffith greatly admired Maud and he was delighted that she was willing to contribute to his paper. She was even persuaded to smuggle passports for Irishmen to Paris to enable them to go to South Africa to fight against the British.

As if she had not enough to do, Maud, still leaving Iseult in Paris with her nanny, sailed again to America for another short, but exhausting tour, to speak on behalf of the Boers. One might wonder how this matter would impinge on American foreign policy but yet she felt that the Irish Americans, at least, should have further ammunition with which to bombard the British, especially in this time of difficulty. Never was that famous phrase, England's difficulty is Ireland's opportunity, more apt.

The Daughters of Erin – Inghinidhe na hEireann

Of all the organisations with which Maud Gonne was involved, it was probably this particular one for which she is most remembered. Ask people in these early 21st century days about Maud and they would probably know of the Daughters of Erin. When she was ignominiously excluded from the male dominated societies and clubs in Dublin, Maud determined that women, too, would have their say. And so it was that women flocked to join the various branches of the Inghinidhe not only in Dublin itself but in towns and villages throughout the island. The women debated the serious issues of the day and, as only women could and would do, they set about being of practical help to those who needed such assistance. For example many branches set up classes for children allowing them to participate in all sorts of youthful activities.

Then, in 1900, another women's organisation, Cumann na nGaedheal, was formed to give women further opportunities to air their views. This was an immensely successful grouping which, in due course, absorbed the Inghinidhe into it in 1911 when Irishwomen were getting more and more active in Nationalist politics.

Maud Gonne's path to immortality in Irish eyes was making further steady progress.

The McBride connection

An Irishman from Westport in county Mayo in the west of Ireland, John McBride, had made a name for himself during the Boer War. Having enlisted as a British soldier he soon saw, at least in his Irish eyes, the senselessness, indeed the treachery, of joining in a cause that was similar to the plight of the Irish. He decided to change sides and went over to the Boers. This in itself could have been of no particular note as this type of desertion is not unknown in times of war. But McBride, in great admiration for the feats of the Boer generals, was determined to add to their number. He found many captured British soldiers in prisoner of war camps who were Irishmen and he put it to them that they should not be fighting for the British but should be opposing them. As a consequence, many converted to his idea and the Irish Brigade was created. The Brigade fought valiantly in many of the famous battles of the campaign and won many plaudits, not to mention medals, from the grateful Boers. The war in the end went against them but they had engaged the mighty British for three years at a time when the Empire could ill afford to fight such a war in such a faraway place.

McBride returned to Europe and domiciled for a time in France. He was, of course, forbidden to enter Britain or Ireland on pain of arrest. In Paris Maud met this hero, John McBride. Like so many other listeners, she was in awe of his bravery and determination. McBride soon set off for America to spread his story there. Maud accompanied him encouraged by her Dublin friend, Arthur Griffith.

It was whilst in America that McBride proposed to Maud that they should marry. It might have seemed an auspicious suggestion now that Millevoye was no longer on the scene and that she was still managing to keep Willie Yeats at arms' length. But, when they returned to Paris, everyone with any love for and interest in Maud advised against the marriage. Iseult was opposed as was even John McBride's mother. Her sister, Kathleen was against the union as well as Griffith. But all theses views were set aside and Maud married McBride on 21 February 1903. She was then 36 and her husband 35.

It was not long before Maud realised her mistake. McBride was a heavy drinker and an inattentive spouse. Maud even confided in her mystical Yeats that she was unhappy. Then she discovered that she was pregnant and her son, Jean Seagan (later to be changed to Sean) was born on 26 January 1904. In the interim, and before the child's birth, she had returned to Dublin to get involved in more anti-royalist protests, this time in connection with King Edward's visit to the city.

Despite the fact that her marriage had certainly been ill-conceived, Maud was overjoyed at Sean's arrival. She had just bought a house at Colleville in Normandy from the proceeds of a legacy left to her by her late great aunt Augusta, with whom she had stayed for a time in her early childhood. This meant that she and her little family had another bolthole to retreat to at times of stress.

Stress there was aplenty. She filed for divorce but, of course, there was no such thing for Roman Catholics. However, early in 1906 after she had left her husband for over a year, an acrimonious divorce was played out in court and she was at last free from the man she freely acknowledged she should never have married. As an interesting aside her half sister, Eileen, fell in love with, and married, Joseph McBride, the elder brother of John. Unlike Maud's short and unhappy marriage, Eileen and Joseph were happily married for many years and had five children.

A French exile

It seems strange to talk of any stay for Maud in France as an exile since she was in residence there on many occasions thus far in her life. But it was now for a very extended period that Maud, Iseult and Sean remained in France and made it their permanent home for ten years from 1906. This was a happy family time for Maud and her children, moving, as they did, between their flat in Paris and their country home in rural Normandy.

However she did not forget Ireland and her Irish connections. She kept in touch with her women friends in the Inghinidhe in Dublin. She engaged in Irish activities in Paris for there was a strong group of Irish émigrés in that city. She became involved in an organisation called the Society of St Patrick and Sean was soon involved in this as well as a little boy.

Willie Yeats continued to visit Maud in Paris in the hope, one would expect, that she would finally accept his own marriage proposal. She relentlessly refused although their relationship persisted. They may indeed have had a brief sexual affair around 1909 but Willie's fervent advances were always rebuffed. In reality theirs was a kind of spiritual marriage.

Her Irish friends, doubtless missing the drive and strength of mind of their colleague, Maud, wrote to inform her of their intention to publish another newspaper *Woman of Ireland*. Helena Moloney, a doughty campaigner in the image of Maud herself, encouraged Maud to write articles for the new paper and she happily obliged. Although resident firmly on the continent, people in Dublin still felt that they had their celebrated Maud in their midst, even if it only meant reading her stories in the paper. In her writings for this paper Maud would have expressed her concern for the continued troubles afflicting the Irish and she would doubtless have informed her Dublin readers of similar problems for the poor of Paris when severe flooding caused havoc for many of its citizens least able to assist themselves. It goes without saying that Maud threw herself into the rescue missions emanating from this local disaster.

Although spending the majority of her time in France, Maud did manage to visit Ireland on a couple of occasions in 1910. She spent time in the west of Ireland on holiday and then returned to Dublin to involve herself in yet another worthy campaign.

In England young children were entitled to the provision of free meals in primary schools. This right did not extend to Ireland although, of course, all were under the same parliament at Westminster at that time. Maud took up the cudgels on the youngsters' behalf along with many other parliamentarians and people of influence through the country. It is interesting to note that another Westminster MP, one James Craig, a member from county Down and in a few short years to become Prime Minister of Northern Ireland, was an ardent campaigner for the exact same right. Not only did he fight for meals for children, he also insisted on provision for adequate heating in country schools throughout Ireland – a campaign he eventually succeeded in having implemented despite fierce opposition from MPs in parliament and from the hierarchy of the Roman Catholic church. Little did people in Ireland realise that these two such opposites, Maud Gonne and James Craig, were fighting for a similar goal. Such are the idiosyncrasies of Ireland's political past. In the meantime Maud helped in setting up canteens and feeding needy youngsters in poverty stricken parts of Dublin.

At home in France in 1913, Maud heard of the 'Lock Out' when poorly paid dock workers were locked out of their jobs by their cynical and heartless employers. Conditions for these men's families were desperate and Maud, along with her friend, Constance Markievicz, engrossed herself in providing food and clothing for the thousands left virtually destitute. Despite her committed crusade, the employers won and the poor employees were forced to return to work (and pledge never to join a union) at a reduced pay. For Maud and her colleagues it was a matter of learning that all dedicated work does not always end in success. It was a hard lesson to learn.

Back in France at the outbreak of World War One, Maud and Iseult busied themselves in nursing injured soldiers returning from the front. It was yet another chastening time for both of them. Whilst away from Paris, probably at Colleville, Maud learned of the Easter Rising. It probably filled her with a deal of pride which soon changed to feelings of pain and despair when she learned of the death of her friend, James Connolly, before a firing squad. Soon she was to hear of the death, again by execution, of John McBride. She had not known of any expected rising and the death of her former husband came as a frightful shock to her. But she was at least able to tell her son, Sean, that his father had died for Ireland. He had never been a good parent to his child but now that he had entered the hallowed halls of Ireland's martyrs, it certainly would be worth recalling that the husband of the heroine, Maud Gonne, was one of those who had suffered the supreme sacrifice in front of a firing squad for the future of mother Ireland.

When the war was over, so too was the long drawn out relationship between Maud and Willie Yeats. For one last time Yeats pleaded with Maud to marry him. For one final time she declined his offer and, in despair but perhaps even of hope, he asked Iseult to become his wife. She also refused. Maud encouraged Yeats, probably for the thousandth time to find another to marry him. In 1918 aged 53 he asked a lovely young Englishwoman, Georgie Hyde-Lees, then in her 20s, to marry him and, for the first time heard the word 'Yes'. Two children were born of that union, Anne, in 1919, and, in 1921, Michael who became a lifelong friend of Brian Faulkner who was to become the sixth and last Prime Minister of Northern Ireland.

Return to Ireland
Not long before the end of the war, Maud and her family came back to the British Isles. Of course they had hoped to go direct to Dublin but, such was Maud's notoriety, she was forbidden to enter Ireland. In February 1918 Maud felt she

could wait no longer. She was impatient to get back to her beloved Ireland. In disguise, with Iseult and Sean in tow, she returned and bought a house, not in some anonymous side street in Dublin, but on fashionable St Stephen's Green. There she carefully renewed many of her old acquaintances and Sean, now aged 14, joined Constance Markievicz's Fianna Scouts.

But 1918 was a bad year to be in Ireland. There was the conscription crisis which she opposed along with most other people of all shades of opinion and then came the so-called German plot. This spooked the authorities and wholesale arrests were made. They had obviously known of Maud's return to the city and she was one of many to be arrested. She was taken not to an Irish jail but to Holloway prison in London. There she languished, disconsolate and ill at ease, to await news from outside. When it came it was not what she wanted to hear. Within a short time of each other, Lucien Millevoye and her sister, Kathleen, had both died. Kathleen is said to have given up when she had heard of the death of her eldest son in the war in Europe. Eventually Maud was released and came back to her family in Dublin.

At length the war was over and the 'khaki' election had returned a vast majority of 'Sinn Fein' MPs who refused to take their seats at Westminster. Life in Nationalist circles was becoming more of the physical force variety and Maud, hero-worshipped as she had often been, now found herself more isolated from those in power. She now sought change for Ireland by constitutional means and not by force. Her son Sean had, on the contrary and unbeknownst to his mother, taken the opposite stance and had joined the IRA. There he led an active service unit during the War of Independence (the so-called Black and Tan war or the Anglo Irish war) and was regularly arrested or was on the run. Maud thought he was studying law, which was not the case at this time, but later in life he did qualify and became a lawyer of some repute.

During the years of the Anglo Irish war (1919-1921) Maud was given the opportunity to act as a judge in the 'Sinn Fein' courts and there performed a most satisfactory job of her new found responsibility.

Then it came the turn of her daughter, Iseult, to choose a husband. Aged 25 she married the 17 year old student, Francis Stuart, on 6 April 1920. Maud was not pleased with the marriage and relations between Francis and Maud were forever strained. The young couple had a daughter, Dolores, who sadly died aged just 3 months of spinal meningitis. In 1926 and 1931 their two other children, Ion and Kay, were born. Maud loved her grandchildren and, in some ways, she was reconciled with her son-in-law through them. He went on to live until February 2000 when he died aged 97. Iseult died in 1954, aged 60.

When the Anglo Irish war ended after the truce of July 1921, Ireland's future still looked unsettled. In October 1921 Treaty talks took place between a very inexperienced Irish team led by Arthur Griffith and the youthful Michael Collins and the highly expert British team led by Lloyd George, Churchill and Birkenhead. The outcome was that the Irish, much to Eamon de Valera's chagrin and disgust, signed the treaty. They had not got everything that they had wanted but sufficient to make progress. In London one of Collins's ADCs had been the 17 year old Sean McBride. The treaty was vehemently debated in the Dail on either side of Christmas 1921 and the pro-treaty side just managed, by 64 votes to 57, to win the day. All six women TDs voted against the treaty (including Constance Markievicz) yet, at least in the early days, Maud was described as being rather neutral in regard to the treaty. However she eventually went into the opposing camp especially after the death of her friend, Arthur Griffith, who died suddenly on 12 August 1922.

Ireland continued in turmoil during 1922 and many of the anti-treaty men took the law into their own hands. Sean McBride took the same line and joined Rory O'Connor in the captured Four Courts garrison in April 1922. When the Free State government, led by Griffith and Collins, blasted the Four Courts men out of their stronghold in the last days of June, Sean was one of the occupants to be arrested and imprisoned in Mountjoy prison. He was soon joined in custody there by his brother-in-law, Francis Stuart.

Although she hardly approved of the actions of Sean and Francis, Maud was soon engaged in yet another 'cause celebre'. Desirous of assisting the men in prison, she set up, with the help of the great campaigner Charlotte Despard, the sister of Lord French, the viceroy no less, the Women's Prisoners Defence League. Much sterling work was carried out on behalf of the men incarcerated in the city's jails by Maud and Charlotte and the indefatigable members of their League. By now Maud was regularly suffering the indignities of having her home searched and wrecked by members of the Crown forces. She was literally in the firing line yet she never gave in to brute force. Her standing in Nationalist circles continued to rise.

In the difficult days after the formation of the two Irish states, Maud and Charlotte bought a house, Roebuck House, in the south Dublin suburb of Clonskeagh where they set up a kind of cooperative. Men and women were taken on and they set up various teams of people to make and mend and even involved themselves in a jam making business. These endeavours, whilst not entirely successful, nonetheless offered those who needed help and a bit of employment a certain outlet for their energies. The authorities, of course, kept a vigilant eye on the Roebuck House goings-on and once Maud was arrested and sent to Kilmainham Jail for 20 days.

In 1926 Sean married Kid Bulfin shortly after he too had been in custody and then on the run. He was even a suspect following the assassination of Kevin O'Higgins in July 1927, which occurred just a few days before the death of Maud's dear friend, Constance Markievicz.

From time to time Maud would hear of Willie Yeats although they probably did not meet. He had taken the treaty side and was now a senator in the Irish Upper House. Sean and Maud continued to oppose the government of WT Cosgrave and even joined a new party, Comhairle na Poblachta, which only lasted a short time before collapsing. Sean was in prison again in 1929 whilst his mother and Charlotte Despard continued to flout government announcements. By 1932 Cosgrave's government had fallen and de Valera and his Fianna Fail party had gone into government for the first time.

The last two decades

In 1932 the friends of Maud made her a presentation to commemorate fifty years of her service to Ireland. She, more than any, had fearlessly and continuously given her help and assistance to all sorts of worthy causes from famine work in Donegal, to helping prisoners, to imparting the Irish story to Irishmen all over the world. No one deserved the accolade more than Maud Gonne. She was another of those idealistic women who, despite not having been born in Ireland, had nonetheless spared nothing of herself in her endeavours to promote a free and independent country.

Charlotte Despard and Maud parted company in 1933 as they had simply wanted to go their different ways. Maud bought over Charlotte's share in Roebuck House and Charlotte, determined to plough a new furrow even when she was in her nineties went to Northern Ireland to live, firstly in Belfast and then to Whitehead in county Antrim where she died in 1939.

Maud's family was growing with the arrival of Sean's children, Anna and Tiernan. By the mid 1930s both Maud and Sean were ardent IRA supporters although her efforts to get elected to local government failed in 1936. Maud continued to dislike de Valera and she considered his 1937 constitution to be very anti-women and gratuitously offensive to them.

In 1938, presumably encouraged by her friends and associates, she wrote the first part of what was a very vague, and some might say coy, autobiography. It asked more questions than it gave answers and there was no mention, of course, about her relationship with Lucien Millevoye. She must have thought her readers very naïve especially when they knew of Iseult's existence, yet revealing nothing about her father. She promised to complete the story one day but never did. She gave her autobiography the alluring title *Servant of the Queen*.

During the first year of the Second World War she lost two of her greatest friends, Willie Yeats and Charlotte Despard. As far as the war was concerned Maud would have been, if anything, pro-German although this hardly mattered as the Free State quietly moved through the conflict as a neutral. De Valera's euphemistic name for it was 'the Emergency'. Her son-in-law, however, became a much more active champion of the Nazi regime and spent most of the war in Germany where he fell in love with a German woman whom he eventually married in 1954 after Iseult's death. His name, even in Ireland today, still causes hackles to rise. Many consider him a traitor to his country whilst others take the more philosophical view that he had every right to choose sides. Unlike that other notorious Irishman,

William Joyce, Lord Haw-Haw, Stuart did not advocate the right wing and purely malicious sentiments of Joyce.

By the conclusion of the war Sean had finally finished his law degree which he ought to have completed many years previously and became a senior counsel at the Irish Bar. More importantly, in terms of his service to Ireland, he became a politician, formed his own party, Clann na Poblachta, and became a minister in Costello's rainbow coalition government of 1948 which, by the determination and endeavours of no less than five parties working together, expelled the administration of Eamon de Valera. It may only have lasted three years until 1951 but it is a government which will be remembered for Sean McBride's participation. He went on to win the Nobel Peace Prize in 1974 and is remembered to this day for his 'McBride Principles'. He died in 1987, aged 83.

After a long and thoroughly eventful life serving Irish men and women throughout the world, Edith Maud Gonne McBride died in Dublin on 27 April 1953 at the age of 86 and was buried in the Republican plot at Glasnevin cemetery. Her name will live on in Ireland and she will surely be recalled as one of the few women in Ireland's history who faced up the men – and won.

Suggested reading

1. Brady, Margery, *The Love Story of Yeats and Maud Gonne*, Cork, 1990.
2. Cardozo, Nancy, *Lucky Eyes and a High Heart – the Life of Maud Gonne*, Indianapolis, 1978.
3. Coxhead, Elizabeth, *Daughters of Erin*, London, 1965.
4. Jordan, Anthony J., *The Yeats Gonne Triangle*, Westport, 2000.
5. Levenson, Samuel, *A Biography of Yeats' Beloved Maud Gonne*, New York, 1976.
6. MacBride, Maud Gonne, *A Servant of the Queen*, Gerrards Cross, 1994.
7. Ward, Margaret, *Maud Gonne – a Biography*, London, 1990.

Constance Markievicz

Feisty Firebrand

During the difficult years of the 19th century, especially after the Great Famine which decimated Ireland's population, many of the Anglo Irish landlords took the opportunity to despatch most of their tenants to north America. Sadly many of these impoverished people died before they ever arrived in the New World. These uncaring members of the gentry gave a bad name to many others who remained in the country to give the best possible chances to those families who lived on their great estates. One such benevolent landlord was Sir Henry Gore-Booth of Lissadell in county Sligo. Whilst some of his neighbours were filling little wooden ships with their own tenants at ports in the west of Ireland, Sir Henry was doing all he could to care for the Lissadell people's needs. He and his wife spent their time feeding them and making sure that their rents were reduced to enable them to remain in their homes. His dedication was legendary and his name was always remembered for his good works.

Sir Henry was the fifth baronet who married Georgina, a daughter of Lord Scarborough. They had a happy married life which produced five children. Their first child, Constance, was born on 4 February 1868. Within the next ten years, their four remaining children, Josslyn, Eva, Mabel and Mordaunt, were born. Of all their offspring the one most remembered in Ireland still to this day is Constance. Even as a child she showed signs of a singular propensity to greatness; even as a young girl Constance showed boldness and audacity. When she rode to hounds early in her life she would not countenance defeat. She was a brilliant horsewoman who usually left every other rider far in her wake. Her passion for riding was renowned and the weekly hunts in county Sligo were events never to be missed. But Constance had another obsession, one most unusual for a girl in her position. She loved to visit and help the tenants on her father's estate. Whenever she could not be found the cry would go out to the servants – 'Go and find Miss Constance'. She would be with a woman who had just had a child or with another elderly tenant who needed some care and attention. In many ways this deep commitment to the needs of those less fortunate than herself was to become the trademark of her entire life.

She did, of course, still live the typical Anglo ascendancy life with regular visits to her parents' home in London. She was even presented to Queen Victoria in 1887 during the monarch's golden jubilee. But she had a great dislike for London and much preferred being back in the grounds of Lissadell.

An unusual choice of career
Most gentry parents looked forward to the day when their teenage daughters would choose a suitable local member of their own class to marry. This however was not to be the case for the feisty Constance. Whilst she did have a number of ardent suitors, she rebuffed them one by one. Her parents, whilst not actually despairing for their eldest daughter's future, were concerned about what would happen to her. When she declared that she wanted to be an artist they initially

baulked at the suggestion but soon, knowing of Constance's determination, they acquiesced. They did know of her interest in art and painting and had seen some of the work which she had done in her earlier years. Constance chose to attend one of the finest art schools in London, the Slade, and there she remained from 1893 until 1897 and, in this period, she met many influential and distinguished artists. And she was making progress in her new career. Many thought her work better than good and she continued to make positive impressions on those around her.

She then decided to move to Paris to the equally renowned Academie Julian and there she met, in 1899, one Casimir Dunin Markievicz, a Polish painter who was also a nobleman whose young wife and younger son had recently died. He had another son with him, Stanislas. Casimir was just 25 years old when Constance was already 31. Romance blossomed and they decided to get married. But this was not going to be a conventional marriage. Constance's parents were unhappy and very uncertain about their daughter's choice of husband. To begin with he was a Roman Catholic and a widower to boot. And then he already had a son in tow. They discussed the situation with Constance but her mind was made up. Sadly, in the early part of 1900, Sir Henry died. He was a relatively young man only in his 50s but he had been worn out by his strenuous travels to the Arctic Ocean where he had journeyed on a number of occasions. Lady Gore-Booth, knowing Constance's strong will and determination, accepted the reality. And so, on 29 September 1900, Casimir married Constance in St Marylebone's Church of England in London and then in the local registry office. The wedding was low key owing to the recent death of her father.

Constance and her husband returned to Dublin where Casimir was introduced to all Constance's friends and acquaintances. He seemed to like it there and was even more pleased to hear that Constance was pregnant. She herself was delighted if a little apprehensive. The doctors advised that the birth could be complicated so Constance repaired to Lissadell. There she was surrounded by her mother and by the house staff. And, even more importantly, there were plenty of able doctors to assist her at the time of delivery. Thus it was that on 13 November 1901 her daughter, Maeve Alyss, was born. The birth, as predicted, had been difficult but she was in good hands. The baby's parents remained at Lissadell for some time and Maeve was baptised at Lissadell Parish Church on 11 January 1902. By this time their little family had been complemented by 7 year old Staskou. He was greatly loved by Constance and he found it easy, or as easy as could be expected, to settle into his new surroundings.

Lady Gore-Booth then took a fateful decision. She agreed to look after Maeve whilst her parents headed off to the Ukraine to visit the Markievicz relatives. They stayed there for nearly six months in 1902 and again returned for a second sojourn in 1903. After that Constance never returned to the home of her in-laws. However it should be said that she did get on well with her new family who found Constance a complete breath of fresh air. To Casimir's mother, her new daughter-in-law was a total surprise, not the sober and restrained child of a typical Anglo Irish family, but a lively and quite eccentric young woman. They liked each other from the start.

When they eventually took up residence in Dublin once more, in a house given to them by Lady Gore-Booth, arrangements had to be made for Maeve and Staskou. The youngsters stayed in Dublin until 1908 off and on, but by then Constance's life had turned upside down. She had continued to keep in with the Castle set and attended balls and soirees with Casimir. Both of them, as distinguished painters, had displayed their work in various exhibitions. Both were still accepting commissions and were moving around the city into the homes of the great and good. They were both popular, although Casimir had taken to drinking, and they involved themselves not only in the art world but also in the ever burgeoning field of acting and the theatre. As the year went by, however, their unconventional lifestyle rather caught up with them and they started to drift apart. Their loyalties appeared to be elsewhere – for Constance particularly. Life really took an about turn. Her focus turned towards Irish politics – and Nationalist ones at that.

A life in politics
It was unusual for a woman to become involved in politics; it was remarkable for a woman with an Anglo Irish background to immerse herself in Nationalist politics; the conversion, however, unbelievable as it appeared, was total and genuine. Many friends of Constance were not really surprised. They had always recognised her stubborn and eccentric streak and so they accepted her change of heart.

By 1908 Constance was a free spirit. Maeve was being comfortably looked after by her mother and Casimir was content in his new circle of artistic friends in the city. She grasped her new found way of life with both hands. She knew instinctively that she would never look back. And she never did.

Entering the world of politics was difficult at the best of times. For a woman to take this step into male dominated circles was momentous even; for an ascendancy woman to even contemplate such a move was unheard of. Yet Constance came, she saw and she conquered. There was no turning back. Her first influence was none other than the founder of Sinn Fein itself, Arthur Griffith. She listened to what he had to say and liked his thoughts and ideas. She always admired him but, in the long run, did not entirely trust him. She wanted to participate in the various clubs and debating societies in the city to further and deepen her knowledge. But she was barred from these groups, not because she was from a gentry background but because she was a woman. There was, however, another female firebrand in the city of Dublin, Maud Gonne. She had come across the same male prejudices and had set up an organisation dedicated to women. This was the Daughters of Erin or, in Irish, Inghinidhe na Eireann. Constance joined immediately and was soon engaged in writing articles for their own paper and encouraging more and more women to get involved. She made a great success of her work with these women.

She now flung herself into Sinn Fein itself and became a member in 1908. There she met Bulmer Hobson, a northern Quaker who was soon to become a very good friend of Constance's. She even was elected as a member of the Sinn Fein executive committee, rather to the chagrin of her old mentor, Arthur Griffith. Constance Markievicz's name was on everyone's lips. She then thought it advisable to join the Gaelic League with the chief objective to learn the Irish language. But here she failed. She found it a very complicated tongue to learn and had to admit defeat. And, if truth be told, she thought those involved to be boring and dull. She may not have succeeded in this endeavour but nothing was going to get in her way of total absorption in her chosen brand of politics.

After James Connolly, that exciting socialist and trades union figure, had returned to Ireland in 1910, Constance was one of the first to find his views clear and unambiguous. She liked what she heard from Connolly's lips and became his disciple. She was to remain totally committed to his ideas for the rest of his life. She was now finding herself mixing with many of the people who were soon to make a name for themselves. She encountered Tom Clarke, the old dynamiter, and the scholarly Patrick Pearse. She even took time off to go to Manchester where her sister, Eva, lived. There she involved herself in a campaign to better the wages and conditions for barmaids and, in a Westminster by-election there, helped defeat none other than Winston Churchill.

A magnificent achievement
Arguably Constance's greatest success came in 1909. Like so many others in Dublin she had noted the immediate positive impact of Lord Baden Powell's Boy Scout Movement. He had started back in 1907 to bring boys together to enjoy the outdoor life. Soon Scout troops were forming all over the world and so Scouting came to Dublin. Constance, however, had other thoughts in her mind. Scouting and the gathering together of lads in patrols also appealed to her and she set about organising an alternative type of organisation. They too would camp and learn tracking skills but she thought they should, of all things, learn to shoot. Her plans met with a great deal of initial opposition, not only from parents and assorted adults, but also from boys themselves. But with the help of her friend Bulmer Hobson, who had actually already tried out some similar activities with boys, Constance persevered. Her first troops started to meet in Dublin and in other towns and villages throughout Ireland. It became an outstanding success. To begin with the boys were not keen on having a woman in charge of their new organisation far less an Anglo Irishwoman. But it was not long before they realised the strength of her tenacity and they joined in droves. And she even did teach them to shoot. It so happened that there was an existing law which permitted this activity on private ground and, as she owned a cottage at Ballaly on the southern outskirts of Dublin, they soon were undertaking some primitive camping skills and learning

to fire weapons. Constance, who throughout her life had a great affinity with boys, greatly enjoyed her latest pursuit.

Over the next years the Fianna Eireann, as she styled her Scouts, flourished and many of her former boys were to take part in, and lose their lives in, the 1916 Easter Rising, Con Colbert and Sean Heuston to name but two and then Liam Mellowes and Joe McKelvey in the aftermath of the rebellion.

Constance, in today's parlance, was 'on a roll'. To give her lads even more excitement she sold her home at Rathmines and moved to a tumbledown house with seven acres at Belcamp Park at Raheny. She set up a commune there and set about trying to convert it for her needs and the purposes of the Scouts. The experiment did not work out and in fact turned out to be an abject failure. After only a few short months she had to return to civilisation in Dublin with her tail between her legs. But being Constance she simply looked at that experiment as part of life's rich tapestry. Nonetheless her Scouting movement continued for some years to come although the Baden Powell Scouts continue to flourish to this day.

1911 and onwards
Her family life was, by now, only hanging together by a thread. Whilst she doubtless still loved her husband, her daughter and her stepson, they now rather slipped out of her life. Maeve remained at Lissadell with her indulgent grandmother; Staskou was packed off to school in Gorey, county Wexford and Casimir lived the good life in Dublin. Constance still performed in a number of stage plays at the Dublin theatres and Casimir would have, on occasion, joined her there. Christmas breaks, at least until 1913 or so, were taken at Lissadell where the family could at least have some time together. But after that Casimir returned to the Ukraine and Constance became more and more immersed in Nationalist activities and politics.

Constance was soon to meet Jim Larkin, the Liverpool born trade unionist and gifted orator. He regularly fought for the cause of the lowly paid workers in Dublin. Constance became good friends with Jim and she admired the work that Larkin was doing in the face of heavy odds. She had now come to consider both Larkin and James Connolly as perhaps her closest friends. They seemed strange bedfellows – she from an ascendancy background and they from poor ones. This was, of course, one of Constance's greatest assets, her ability to form relationships with people who thought the same way as she did, totally regardless of their antecedents.

In August 1911 she was arrested for the first, but certainly not for the last, time. She was generally making a nuisance of herself especially during the coronation visit of King Edward. Little did His Majesty realise that one of the pretty debutantes who had been presented to his late mother in earlier days was now one of his fiercest opponents. In these days Constance began to be considered a good, if not a brilliant, orator. She was getting plenty of practice for she ensured that she was in the middle of any disturbance in Dublin and was always speaking on behalf of the Daughters of Erin and for her Fianna. Everyone was talking about Constance Markievicz but not always for the right reasons.

She went to live at Surrey House, Rathmines on the south side of the city. This was to become her last home. It was the centre of all her varied activities and, as such, was often raided and wrecked by Crown forces. From this base she gave valuable assistance to those who had been expelled from their workplaces during the infamous 'Lock Out' in 1913. The poorly paid dock workers and many of their fellows had, with the encouragement of Jim Larkin, struck for higher wages. They were not being unreasonable with their demands, perhaps just pressing for another shilling per week. But the employers, led by the inscrutable Martin Murphy, were a much greater force than had been anticipated. For six long months up to 20,000 employees were locked out and most of their families all but starved. Had it not been for the dedicated hard work of Constance and others, they would not have survived. The ladies, led with vigour by Madame, as Constance had become known, fed and clothed those who needed help. They took over the kitchens at Liberty Hall, the headquarters of Larkin and the trades unionists, and there they provided a non-stop service of soup, sandwiches and every type of food imaginable. Constance still had at least a tenuous contact with her former wealthy friends and she browbeat them to contribute whatever food was needed. Few people realise how long and arduous this operation went on. But Constance was always there for she was a worker and not a talker as has been so often seen. When the strike was eventually ended she was presented with an illuminated scroll from the poor women of the city in appreciation for the strenuous efforts she had made on their behalf. It became one of her most treasured possessions. And what happened to the workers? Rather than winning their reasonable request for that extra shilling, they had to make do with getting their jobs back and receiving one shilling less in the meagre pay packets.

Soon afterwards her friend, Jim Larkin, dejected at his failure on behalf of the workers, left Ireland and went to America. He did his best to help downtrodden people there but inevitably fell foul of the law and ended up, for a considerable time, as a prisoner in the notorious Sing Sing prison. His good work, however, was carried on by James Connolly who had himself been away from Dublin for a time. He returned to Dublin from working for the trades unions in Belfast where there had been strife, riots, murders and mayhem. Connolly had been in Dublin for the 'Lock Out' and, to prevent the expelled workers from being beaten up by the police and military, had established his Irish Citizen Army with the specific objective of protecting them from often vicious attacks. This organisation, with never more than 300 men and women, was to conduct itself with honour in the Easter Rising which was still to come. Needless to say one of the first recruits to this Irish Citizen Army was Constance Markievicz, soon to become one of the Army's joint treasurers.

By the end of 1913 the Irish Volunteers had been formed and quickly as many as 180,000 had joined. Many said that their major inspiration was Edward Carson and his Ulster Volunteers in the north. Many also said that the inspiration of the southern organisation was heavily influenced, and even inspired, by the Ulstermen who had, in April 1914, brought in arms with which to defend themselves perhaps even against their own beloved Empire. To the Irish Volunteers, led by the scholarly academic, Eoin MacNeill, it appeared infinitely better to see an Ulsterman with a rifle than an Irish Volunteer without one.

Gun running, the First World War and the Easter Rising

Life in Dublin was now incredibly dangerous and complicated and, for Constance, even more so. She was totally involved in all the organisations she had joined and founded – the Daughters of Erin, the Fianna, the Irish Citizen Army and membership of Sinn Fein. She was now totally uninvolved with her family and daughter up in Sligo and with her husband who was now about to join the Russian Army in faraway Ukraine. When she heard that the Irish Volunteers had landed arms at Howth at the end of July 1914, she was thrilled. She was not, however, all that overjoyed when she had not been invited to be there when the arms were unloaded from Erskine Childers' yacht, the *Asgard*. But she did, at least, secretly hide a quantity of the weapons at her Ballaly house where, in recent years, she had taught her Scouts to fire rifles.

Early in September, barely a week after the Howth guns had been landed, the world conflict broke out. Everyone wondered where the Volunteers would stand. Whilst many refused to join the British and Allied forces, many thousands did, and with the active encouragement of the leader of the Irish Parliamentary Party, John Redmond. Constance, like so many others, was concerned by this split in the Volunteers. She herself was opposed to Irishmen joining up and she did what she could to discourage enlistment. Members of her own family, however, did join up and many died.

By the early days of 1916, when the war was well into its second year, rumours of a rebellion emerged. Active members of the Volunteers probably considered that this was the time to rise up against the British. The age old axiom, 'England's difficulty is Ireland's opportunity', was on their lips. The Volunteers, and separately the Irish Citizen Army, were regularly to be seen marching up and down the streets of Dublin. In January James Connolly declared that if nothing happened, he would take his Army and line them up against the vast power of the British forces. This was deemed to be a ridiculous statement but a secret group amongst the Volunteers, the so-called Military Council, took Connolly aside, warned him of the foolhardiness of his plan and, it seems, converted him to their cause – which was none other than a rebellion to take place over Easter 1916. Constance Markievicz, like the majority of the leading Volunteers, knew nothing of any proposed plans. For once, in Ireland's recent chequered past, there were only a few 'in the know', thus averting information from being passed to the enemy – the administration at Dublin Castle.

The Easter Rising did break out on Monday 24 April 1916. It had had to be postponed because of the orders from Eoin MacNeill (who was not a member of the Military Council) to countermand Patrick Pearse's orders for manoeuvres on Easter Day. Pearse and the other members of the Military Council, including Connolly and Tom Clarke, decided to proceed for they feared that they would be ridiculed for failing to strike. Constance, when she eventually heard of the action, was asked by Michael Mallin to join him at his command site at St Stephen's Green. She was delighted to do so and turned out smartly dressed in a military uniform complete with a slouch hat. She certainly looked the part and when Mallin appointed her as his second in command she was thrilled. It turned out that she was to be the only commissioned female soldier during the Rising, Dr Kathleen Lynn being the only other commissioned woman though, of course, a medical doctor.

Trying to defend the public park that was St Stephen's Green was impossible. The rebels started to dig trenches which, though sounding ridiculous at the beginning, soon made a little more sense when that type of preparation was prevalent in France on the battlefields of the Somme, for example. Mallin and his company had not made any effort to capture any of the high buildings surrounding the park such as the Shelbourne Hotel. By failing in this objective Mallin's rebels were soon unceremoniously chased out of the park by withering gunfire from British officers who were in the hotel at the time. In less than 24 hours the group of dishevelled rebels was ensconced in the College of Surgeons at the west end of the Green. For the remainder of Easter week they were pinned down in the college although they did engage in regular sniping at their enemy. What Constance Markievicz thought of the arrangements for the defence of such a poorly chosen location has never been revealed. However it is probably fair to say that she was dismayed at the total lack of preparation for such a momentous venture.

She only had time to think what might have been as she cowered with her associates within the college building. For herself, however, one positive occurrence happened – she felt the urge to convert to Catholicism.

At her court martial Constance had her say and prepared to be sentenced to death just as her friend, James Connolly, had been. She had her wish but then she heard that General Maxwell, the British commander, had commuted her sentence to life imprisonment because she was a woman. This did not please her as she too wanted to die for Ireland as the Rising signatories had done. She was sent to Aylesbury Jail in England and was the only insurgent to be held there. To add insult to injury she was treated as a common criminal and not as a political prisoner. She was extremely lonely although she did receive a few visits from her sister, Eva, who was living in England. In July 1917 Constance was released from prison with the rest of the rebels after a general amnesty. She returned to Dublin as a heroine where the people gave her an ecstatic welcome. It was at this stage that she was finally received into the Roman Catholic Church. As was said at the time – 'Her acceptance of Ireland was as complete as she could make it'. Her journey into nationalism was complete.

When she returned to Dublin she had no home of her own any more. She went to live with the Coghlan family who treated her very well and where she loved every member of that family.

Constance Markievicz – politician

Although over 2,000 men and women had been imprisoned and interned after the Rising – a far greater number than those who actually participated in it – they had, by the time of Constance's release, all been returned to Ireland. Pressure had been brought to bear on the British government to ameliorate their attitude to the rebels and they had been forced, or at least had felt obliged, to set them free. Back in Dublin the Sinn Fein executive held a meeting to elect a committee of 26 members. Constance came out in 5th position with 617 votes which showed her popularity amongst the rank and file. It was interesting to note that Michael Collins only scraped in at 26th with just 340 votes. How fortunes were soon to change. Eamon de Valera was elected President. It had, in some quarters, been expected that Arthur Griffith, the founder of the movement after all, would be chosen but, realising that he was not the man for such a job, stood down in favour of de Valera.

Constance's fame and reputation continued to go before her and, in August 1917, she was given the freedom of her native Sligo. What the Gore-Booths thought of this accolade can only be imagined.

During 1918, with British casualties mounting in Europe as the Great War teetered forward, there came the so-called 'Conscription Crisis' throughout Ireland. In the south the proposition was met with complete opposition. Everyone, from Sinn Fein, the southern Unionists and the Catholic Church, vociferously voiced their condemnation at the proposal to introduce conscription to Ireland and, in the end, the idea was dropped. It meant, however, that the British administration at Dublin Castle was becoming very jittery and in May there came the spurious 'German Plot' and many leaders of Irish Ireland were arrested, including Constance. She was imprisoned at Holloway Jail in London and remained in custody until March 1919. Three of her closest women friends, Maud Gonne, Hanna Sheehy Skeffington and Mrs Tom Clarke were also incarcerated with her. At least this time she had her friends to talk to.

Whilst she was imprisoned Constance Markievicz was elected MP for the St Patrick's division of Dublin in the 'khaki' election of December 1918 when 73 'Sinn Feiners' were chosen by the electorate, leaving only a rump of 6 Irish Parliamentary Party members at Westminster. Constance was thus the first ever woman to be elected to the British House of Commons although she did not take her seat as the 'Sinn Feiners' had declared that, if elected, they would not sit in a 'foreign' parliament. As an amusing aside, Constance did go into the Palace of Westminster at a later date when she was in London just to look at her locker and coat peg emblazoned with her name – Constance Markievicz MP.

In opposition to the British parliament the Sinn Feiners, who were not on the run or in prison at the time and that was only some 20 of them, took their seats for the first session of Dail Eireann on 21 January 1919. That was an auspicious day not only on the account of that inaugural meeting but it was also the day when the War of Independence or the Anglo Irish War or the Black and Tan War broke out. President de Valera was also one of those in jail – he was being held at Lincoln Jail – although, during February, he was 'sprung' from that prison by Michael Collins and some of his accomplices.

When the next Dail met in April both Constance and de Valera were in attendance and, at this session, de Valera appointed Constance as his Minister of Labour and so she became the first woman to be given a seat in a Cabinet, albeit an illegal one. For the next few months she proved to be a most conscientious minister although, like all her colleagues, she was constantly on the run and changing her offices to avoid capture by the resolute members of His Majesty's forces who were on the lookout to arrest as many of the members of the Dail as possible. In June, the Crown forces caught up with her and she was imprisoned, yet again, this time in Cork jail. Her sentence was four months although the conditions on this occasion were much more favourable. But all these terms of imprisonment were beginning to take their toll on the health of Constance. She was, after all, now 51 years old and without recourse to regular medical attention.

Whilst she was undertaking her ministerial job in Dublin de Valera was not in Dublin but in America. He had travelled there in June 1919 and did not return until Christmas 1920. Consequently he missed almost the entire War of Independence and it was Michael Collins who headed the administration under exceedingly difficult circumstances. Constance did keep in touch with de Valera when he was out of the country but, in truth, she never was completely at ease with the 'Chief'.

Life for Constance was incredibly stressful and the situation was not helped in September 1920 when she was again arrested 'for treasonable practices' and sent to Mountjoy Prison. She was there for ten long months until she was released at the time of the truce in July 1921. By now she had spent a total of more than three years in jail. Her experiences in prison were only relieved by letters from her sister, Eva, who had a kind of mystical contact with her older sister. They may not have seen each other very often over the years but there always seemed to be this bond which certainly kept Constance's flagging spirits up. But the fact that she was in prison for a large part of the War of Independence at least kept her safe from the threats that she would doubtless have encountered had she been free during that troubled time.

The Anglo Irish Treaty

When the War of Independence finally came to a conclusion in the summer of 1921 following a spirited appeal from King George V at the opening of the Northern Ireland parliament in Belfast City Hall, an opportunity was given for Eamon de Valera to travel to London for talks with David Lloyd George, the British Prime Minister. These discussions came to nothing although, in October, a further chance was afforded the Irish to enter into meaningful talks to discuss the Free State's future role in its relations with Britain. This time, however, de Valera famously declined to lead the delegation. He sent, amongst other able men, Arthur Griffith and Michael Collins, to hammer out a deal. De Valera knew that he could never achieve what he himself wanted and that was a complete break for the new state from the British yoke.

Consequently the Treaty talks, which started in October and eventually ended on 6 December, agreed on a compromise solution. As Collins said, it was a stepping stone towards an independent Ireland. De Valera was, of course, astounded that his men had signed such a deal but Griffith reminded him that the five negotiators had been sent not just as mere delegates but as full plenipotentiaries who had the right to sign a treaty on behalf of the Free State. After rowdy debates amongst the members of the Dail on both sides of Christmas 1921, the Treaty was accepted by 64 votes to 57. De Valera immediately walked out with all his supporters leaving Griffith to lead the new state into an uncertain future.

And where did Constance Markievicz stand in all this acrimonious discussion? Like all six women deputies she was firmly opposed to any deal with the British and she had therefore stormed out of the Dail with de Valera. Like her leader, she was now very much isolated especially when the country voted by at least three to one to support the Treaty. Constance was now left in the wilderness. Many thought that this might have been a glorious opportunity for her to rest and regain her strength. But this was not what Madame chose to do. She spent time in Paris at the post war Peace Conference where de Valera had thought that the Americans would, as they had vowed, stand up for little nations and give them their backing. But they had not reckoned with President Wilson whose allegiance, in the Irish context, was not with the Irish, but with the British. And anyway their part of the country was not a sovereign government.

Leaving France Constance stopped off in London to visit Eva before travelling to America where she delivered numerous fiery speeches on behalf of the Irish cause. Countess Constance Markievicz was a real draw to the Americans who loved those with titles and more especially with the type of speech-making Constance was able to impart. She was a huge success in many American towns and cities and was in constant demand to speak to Irish American audiences to tell them of the continuing Irish struggle against the British oppressor.

When she returned to Ireland for the elections of June 1922, she, along with a number of her colleagues, lost her seat in the Dail. The ordinary Irish people had spoken. They no longer wanted death, killing and destruction but instead wished to have an opportunity to pursue a peaceful existence. But this was not to be. By the last days of June 1922 and only a few days after the election had been held, the Irish Civil War broke out. Brother now fought against brother and father against son, that which the Irish least wanted had come to pass and with a vengeance. Constance was in her place at the beginning of the conflict with those who opposed the fledgling administration of Griffith and Collins. She fought in the early days in the already devastated Sackville (soon to be O'Connell) Street along with de Valera's right hand man, Cathal Brugha. Although the same Brugha had been frightfully injured during the Easter Rising, and had survived, he now fell dead in a hail of Free State soldiers' bullets within three days of the start of the Civil War.

Constance was soon spirited out of Ireland and went to Glasgow where she edited a weekly paper and continued to address audiences who were anxious to hear of the troubles in Ireland. She also travelled into England to speak wherever she was wanted, always having to keep a step ahead of British agents who were determined to capture her. They did not succeed.

By the end of the Civil War Constance was back in her beloved homeland and was soon re-elected to the Dail for her former St Patrick's constituency. Once more, in November, she was arrested and imprisoned yet again. This time she started a hunger strike and was released before Christmas. Detention in draughty prison cells continued to take its toll on the once spirited Constance. She was beginning to feel her age especially as she had long since lost a home she could call her own.

Those last years

From time to time Constance did give some thought as to what was happening to the other dear members of her family. Casimir had long since been back in eastern Europe and had fought on the Russian side in the war. He had been injured and, although he did survive the conflagration, he was not the man he had been. He returned to Dublin in 1924 and met up with his wife once more. Neither could believe how changed they both were. The years and the struggles to survive had taken their toll yet they still were able to enjoy one another's company for a short while. Casimir had never been able to adjust to Constance's new lifestyle and their separation had become an inevitability.

Constance also made contact with Maeve and they were once more able to go shopping in Grafton Street and spend time tinkering with motor car engines which was an activity close to both their hearts. Constance still had many of her organisations to attend and she even took time to paint once more. But these official duties, which included her efforts to revive the fortunes of her much loved Fianna, began to lose their edge. She now preferred to visit the old and needy in the slums of Dublin and to help them whenever she could. She was becoming more and more dishevelled herself and, if the truth were told, she was beginning to look like one of the poor she was helping.

Sadness pursued her when she heard of the death in June 1926 in England of her dear sister, Eva. She did not attend her funeral because she felt probably a little ashamed and also because she felt the Gore-Booths would be critical of her. There is a poignant story told of her reaction to Eva's passing. Around the time of the funeral Constance was found sitting in a dark back room in the Coghlan's home where she was living, in floods of tears. It was a very private moment which was only disturbed by one of the Coghlan children entering the room not knowing that Constance was there. The once fiery and feisty Constance Markievicz was human after all. She had always been the pillar of strength and now there she sat appreciating her own mortality following upon the death of her sister. For Constance, this was the beginning of the end. All those close to her were drifting apart and she doubtless felt the emptiness of her life at that crucial time.

During the early part of 1927 she reluctantly joined de Valera's new Fianna Fail party. She was elected to the Dail that year yet again and continued to canvass on behalf of those who had elected her although she herself was never to enter the chamber with the other Fianna Fail deputies who still would not sign the oath of allegiance to the British monarch.

In the first days of July 1927, just as Dublin and the Free State government were burying Kevin O'Higgins after his assassination, Constance fell ill. She entered Sir Patrick Dun's hospital and was placed in a public ward as she had no money to be given a private room. Anyway she was much happier with the poor of the city. She was diagnosed with appendicitis and initially made good progress. However her condition started to deteriorate as peritonitis set in and emergency messages were broadcast for her family to come to her bedside. It seems totally incredible that one of those BBC radio broadcasts asking for relatives of a very sick Constance to attend her registered a complete success. Casimir, in distant Ukraine and Staskou out there as well, and Maeve in England, all heard the message and hastened to Dublin. They all were with their wife and mother when Constance died on 15 July 1927 aged just 59. Even telephone calls to the neighbours of the family at Lissadell had summoned them to Dublin.

The funeral of Constance Markievicz was in total contrast to that of O'Higgins just a few days previously. Whilst he had been accorded the full trappings of a State funeral, complete with carriages and top-hatted mourners, the obsequies of a heroine of the Republic were held in entirely different circumstances. The city fathers refused to allow a lying in state in the Mansion House for fear of riots and disturbances. And so Constance was laid in the Rotunda where thousands of the poor and downtrodden of the city respectfully filed past her open coffin. On the Sunday the procession to Glasnevin Cemetery was lined with bare headed friends and acquaintances all along the route. Tears flowed as the cortege passed by – and they were the tears of those whom Constance had helped in her lifetime – those without title or station, simply those who had been in need of her help. Eamon de Valera, in his oration over the grave, intoned – 'Madame Markievicz is gone from us; Madame, the friend of the toiler, the lover of the poor. Ease and station she put aside, and took the hard way of service with the weak and the downtrodden. Sacrifice, misunderstanding and scorn lay on the road she adopted, but she trod it unflinchingly'. De Valera had spoken for the nation. Ireland had surely lost one of its greatest heroines.

The family quietly rode in cars to the graveside that sad day – Maeve, her long abandoned daughter; Casimir, her long suffering husband; Staskou, her much loved stepson and, to his eternal credit, Sir Josslyn Gore-Booth, her true and loving brother.

It is now over 80 years since the death of one of Ireland's greatest heroines. Has Ireland remembered her? A monument of sorts has been erected in St Stephen's Green which hardly gives such a renowned woman the credit she deserves. However, on Easter Monday 2003, a most fitting sculpture was unveiled in the centre of the village of Rathcormack in county Sligo on the main road out of Sligo, close to Drumcliffe, and only a few miles from Constance's childhood home at Lissadell. At last a truly appropriate memorial has been set in place and many thanks and congratulations are due to the Constance Markievicz Millennium Committee for ensuring that this fine Irishwoman is remembered.

Suggested reading
1. Coxhead, Elizabeth, *Daughters of Erin – Five Women of the Irish Renascence*, London, 1965.
2. Haverty, Anne, *Constance Markievicz – an Independent Life*, London, 1988.
3. James, Dermot, *The Gore-Booths of Lissadell*, Dublin, 2004.
4. McGowan, Joe (ed), *Constance Markievicz – the People's Countess*, Mullaghmore, 2003.
5. Markievicz, Constance, *Prison Letters of Countess Markievicz*, London, 1987.
6. Marreco, Anne, *The Rebel Countess – the Life and Times of Constance Markievicz*, London, 1967.
7. Norman, Diana, *Terrible Beauty – a Life of Constance Markievicz*, London, 1987.
8. O'Faolain, Sean, *Constance Markievicz or the Average Revolutionary*, London, 1934.
9. Scoular, Clive, *Maeve de Markievicz – Daughter of Constance*, Killyleagh, 2003.
10. Van Voris, Jacqueline, *Constance de Markievicz – in the Cause of Ireland*, Massachusetts, 1967.

Hanna Sheehy Skeffington

Steadfast Suffragette

Johanna Mary Sheehy (always known as Hanna) was born in Kanturk, county Cork on 24 May 1877, the first of six children, four girls and two boys, of David and Bessie (nee McCoy). Hanna was the only child to be born in county Cork for her father, early in his career, had bought a mill near Templemore in county Tipperary, and the rest of his family was born there. David then went into politics and joined the Irish Parliamentary Party (the IPP). He was elected MP for south Galway in 1885, in the time of C.S. Parnell, and represented this constituency until 1900. Later he became MP for south Meath from 1903 until the decimation of the IPP in 1918 when, with dozens of others, he lost his seat in the so called Sinn Fein landslide in the 'khaki' election of December 1918.

David's interesting life started before he was elected as an MP. By the time of his marriage he was a member of the Irish Republican Brotherhood (the IRB) and had been imprisoned on more than one occasion. He then had to flee to America to save him from the clutches of authority and to prevent further incarceration. His brother, Eugene, who became a priest, was also a prominent member of the IRB and was often at odds with the Roman Catholic hierarchy. He was involved with the Land League and was certainly a militant type of clergyman. In his later life Eugene attended the inaugural meeting of the Irish Volunteers in Dublin in 1913 and fought in the GPO during the ill-fated Easter Rising of April 1916.

And so into this colourful family little Hanna was born in 1877. By the end of the 1880s, when Hanna was 12 years old, the Sheehy clan moved to Belvedere Place in Dublin to live. By now David was an MP and he often invited fellow MPs to his home. Here Hanna and her brothers and sisters had the opportunity to meet many of them like Parnell and even William Gladstone when he had occasion to visit Ireland. It was a wonderful chance for the children to interact with these important men and their appetite for Irish history and politics was well and truly whetted. Even when guests were not in the house Hanna's parents actively encouraged their children to learn about their country's turbulent past and to look forward to an independent Ireland. Hanna especially believed in freeing Ireland from the British yoke by forceful means, if necessary. Her parents and uncle Eugene would, of course, have taken a similar stance although her paternal grandfather tended to be more for change by constitutional methods.

Hanna's schooldays were spent at Eccles Street Dominican convent and she was a brilliant pupil there. When she was 18, in 1895, Hanna contracted TB (a not uncommon occurrence at the time) and, to aid her recovery, she was packed off to various spas in Germany and France to recover. She soon got better and returned home to enter St Mary's College where she continued to be a top student, graduating BA in 1899 and advancing her degree to MA in 1902. In those days, of course, a university education for a girl was almost unheard of and it shows the tenacity and single-mindedness of Hanna to achieve such distinctions. These college days stood her in great stead throughout her life and gave her the strength of character to stand up for herself and her causes for the rest of her life.

Courtship and marriage

During one of the regular gatherings held at the Sheehy home, Hanna met Francis Skeffington. He had spent much of his young life in Downpatrick, county Down, the only child born to his well-travelled 40 year old mother and strict disciplinarian 22 year old father. Francis was an interesting and talented young man to whom Hanna grew ever more and more attached. Some of the favourite topics of discussion at the meetings in her home included that of university education for women and feminism and women's rights. To most men these matters were anathema but Hanna was delighted to hear Francis support her views. He truly believed in equality for women in every aspect of life. Hanna had joined the Irish Association of Women Graduates (whose numbers were unremarkably small) and, for good measure, the Irish Women's Suffrage Association whose leader was the celebrated Mrs Anna Haslam.

In every way Francis gave Hanna his complete approval for what she was doing. She thought he was the kind of man she would like to marry and, on 27 June 1903, she and Francis were wed in the university chapel on St Stephen's Green. They henceforth became known as Mr and Mrs Sheehy Skeffington. It was a gesture of 'equal rights including holding on to your own name' solidarity which probably shocked most of their family and friends. They did not care as they had made their first joint stand together. They made their first home in the suburb of Rathgar.

Hanna settled down to teach at St Mary's College, Donnybrook and at Cabra Dominican convent. She was admired and respected by both pupils and staff alike. Francis became the first lay registrar at University College, Dublin, proving his worth as an able and resourceful man. However he soon resigned the post and took up journalism and writing for whichever paper or magazine would take his articles. He was soon promoting equal rights for women, especially their demand to enter as equals to university.

Hanna, whilst an extremely hard worker, was beginning to suffer from melancholia although she was able to overcome this affliction by sheer hard work and undivided attention to the preparation of her school work. She was also becoming decidedly more forceful and even militant in pursuit of her equal rights campaigns. And her name, and that of her husband, was beginning to be well known throughout Dublin in suffragette circles.

By 1908, when Hanna was not feeling very robust herself, Francis had fallen ill with diphtheria and very nearly died. He went to Youghal in county Cork to recuperate and Hanna moved their home to Rathmines. She continued to be drawn to the suffragette cause and its vibrant militancy and decided it was time to leave Mrs Haslam's lacklustre organisation. She became friendly with James and Gretta Cousins who were leading lights in the to fight for the cause of women's suffrage. So, along with Gretta, Hanna formed their own organisation, the Irish Women's Franchise League, in November 1908. However their group soon became too middle class which resulted in even more Nationalist women, like Constance Markievicz, having nothing to do with Hanna and her League. It turned out to be not a very successful association.

On 19 May 1909, Hanna gave birth to what was to be her only child, a son, Owen. Although both parents had been brought up in the Roman Catholic faith, both Hanna and Francis had long since drifted away from the church and so decided that their son would be raised without any religious content in his young life. And there were other significant family changes. Francis' mother died, aged 80, and his father became overly dependent on his son. Hanna's three sisters all married – Mary to Tom Kettle, Margaret to Frank Culhane and Kathleen to Frank Cruise O'Brien. Hanna was also meeting with the various prominent women in Dublin at this time. She knew Constance Markievicz and Maud Gonne. However, Gonne's women's group, the Daughters of Erin, was not to Hanna's liking and, unlike so many others at that time, she chose not to join. She did, notwithstanding, regularly contribute to many of their good causes, one of which was dear to her heart, the feeding of poor children at school.

The yet more militant Hanna Sheehy Skeffington

By this stage, 1909-1910, Hanna had her mind turned to militant action to further her women's causes. She considered that passive and constitutional advances were making little progress and she, with her husband's full support, moved up a gear with regard to belligerent and more aggressive action. She got to know yet another feisty campaigner, Charlotte Despard, and her Women's Freedom League. Mrs Despard, who was the sister of Lord French, the last Viceroy, was a thorn in the flesh not only to her brother but also to the entire British administration in Dublin. Hanna was impressed by her tactics and so she took her case direct to Westminster where she caused a certain degree of havoc by advocating a boycott of the 1911 census. She then appeared in Belfast in early 1912 when Winston Churchill was in the city to promote Home Rule but who, much to his chagrin, was kept out of the Ulster Hall by the Unionists opposed to Home Rule and forced to speak in a tent in Celtic Park. Hanna tried unsuccessfully to gain entrance to the Ulster Hall herself and had to repair to the tent. Her infamy had gone before her even to Belfast. Becoming more and more militant Hanna found herself in many awkward situations vigorously opposing the stance taken against women.

In May 1912 their Irish Women's Franchise League published the first edition of their own newspaper, the *Irish Citizen*. It was to become a popular eight page weekly which lasted for eight years, considerably longer than many of the papers and broadsheets that were then being circulated. Much of the work in finding articles for the paper fell, of course, to Hanna but she seemed keen to take on these further responsibilities. Her readers over the years were lambasted with the current inanities of the government as she saw them. In 1912 Hanna, both through the paper and by dint of her confrontational behaviour, fought to ensure that votes for women were included in the 1912 third Home Rule bill – but to no avail. So, to draw attention to this slight, Hanna and her friends took to breaking shop windows in Dublin's public buildings and, for her action, she was arrested and sent to prison. She described her first taste of prison life to be 'not too bad at all' and, to ensure that her plight kept to the fore, she went on a hunger strike. The government was always anxious about hunger strikes so they introduced the so-called Cat and Mouse act which meant that she was soon released although she knew that further similar action would see her immediately returned to prison. This time she had been seven days on her hunger strike and thirty days in jail in all. It was during her imprisonment that Prime Minister Asquith visited Dublin only to have his carriage attacked by some of Hanna's friends.

But her militant action was only too soon to have its consequences. She was immediately sacked from her post at her school and, although this proved a most unpopular decision by the authorities, nonetheless she was out of a job. On her release, however, Hanna was not at all repentant and carried on with her outrageous behaviour. Post boxes were set on fire thus keeping her name very much in the public eye. James Connolly, as always very active on the socialist front, approved of Hanna's activities and the two got to know each other quite well. He even addressed one of the Irish Women's Franchise League meetings towards the end of 1913. When Andrew Bonar Law and Edward Carson were visiting Dublin during that year, Hanna was again in trouble. This time she went up to their carriage after breaking through the police cordons and pushed some of their leaflets into their faces. For this crime she was jailed for five days and even went on another hunger strike immediately. She was now not only a well known Dublin character; she had become a notorious one. In the midst of all this rebellious activity, however, Hanna did turn her energies into good works. During the disastrous 'Lock Out' in 1913 she helped regularly in the soup kitchens at Liberty Hall where she often met up with Connolly and Constance Markievicz.

The outbreak of war and the murder of Francis
Many militant women's organisations in Dublin and even Emmeline Pankhurst's suffragettes in London suspended their activities during the First World War and started to help the government in prosecuting the war against Germany. Hanna and her organisation, however, were disgusted at these actions for they felt that this would simply further postpone improved rights for women for even more years. They opposed the war and also any women's help for the war effort. Needless to say this stance shocked people and much opprobrium was poured upon the Irish Women's Franchise League. Hanna could not have cared less and they remained totally anti-war throughout those years 1914-1918.

In 1915 she was chosen to go to Holland as an Irish delegate to an international peace congress but was refused a passport and was not allowed to leave the country.

All the while Francis continued to help his wife and to campaign on behalf of women. He himself was, along with many others it must be said, speaking out against conscription in Ireland. He was arrested and convicted and sent to prison for twelve months. However he immediately commenced a hunger strike and was quickly released. There had been a great deal of public support for Francis and his actions and their demands for his release were effective. Quite soon after he was free once more, Francis was invited to go to America to give lectures. He accepted and was soon making money by telling the Irish Americans of the sufferings of the Irish people; he became a popular speaker. Hanna was not keen that he had gone for his health was never very robust but she made sure to keep in touch with him by letter. She stayed at home looking after Owen, doing a little bit of teaching and, of course, keeping the *Irish Citizen* going. Francis's tour went well and he made a lot of money. He was even offered a job as a journalist but he declined the offer. There were passport difficulties for Francis when he returned to Liverpool about getting back to Ireland but he was eventually allowed to go back in time to spend Christmas 1915 with his family. As the fateful year of 1916 approached, further changes occurred within the family. Two of Hanna's brothers-in-law, Tom Kettle and Frank Cruise O'Brien were fighting in Europe in British uniforms. Tom died at the Somme and was remembered as one of the best known war poets. Frank Culhane had died leaving Margaret a widow with four children.

The Sheehy Skeffingtons, like many other well known people in Dublin, had heard rumours that a rising was imminent. But there was no definite information and, if anyone did know, they were not saying anything. When Easter Monday dawned, after McNeill had countermanded Pearse's Easter Sunday orders, it came as a huge surprise when the rising did break out. When the GPO was captured and the word got out, Hanna felt sure that the insurrection would last whilst Francis was more pessimistic; he said it would be doomed from the start. Francis hurried to Liberty Hall to try to see Connolly but, by midday, the rebels under Pearse and Connolly had left and were making their way to what was to become the centre of operations, the General Post Office – that symbol of British rule in Ireland. Francis did not get to see Connolly, therefore, but he immediately saw trouble brewing in the city. He actually visited the GPO later on the Monday by which time some looting had started in the large shops in Sackville Street. There he managed to see Connolly for a short while but could not persuade him to try to prevent the senseless pillaging of the stores.

Hanna and Francis made up their minds to try to dissuade the poor population not to loot and they went around trying to garner support for an anti-looting civilian force. Hanna herself went to the GPO on the Tuesday which was, to say the least, a very dangerous sortie. Later in the day Hanna met with Francis to discuss the ever deteriorating situation and to decide what to do next. Hanna headed for home to care for 7 year old Owen while Francis hurried off to find more willing volunteers. It was to be the last time that Hanna saw her husband alive.

What happened next was information only found out by Hanna through sheer determination. Francis had been arrested and taken to Portobello Barracks. The next morning he was taken out into the yard along with two respectable journalists, Thomas Dickson and Patrick MacIntyre, and shot dead. The officer who had given the order, Captain J.C. Bowen-Colthurst, was on duty at the barracks when Hanna came in great distress to try to ascertain her husband's whereabouts. Little did she know then that this very man had been responsible for Francis's untimely death. She went home little the wiser, only soon to be confronted at her house by Bowen-Colthurst and sixty of his men who had entered and ransacked the house – presumably looking for evidence against Francis.

The murder of Francis Sheehy Skeffington caused uproar in the House of Commons in London. John Dillon, an MP of the Irish Parliamentary Party, had heard from Hanna all that she knew and the matter was immediately debated at Westminster. Bowen-Colthurst was taken offside and apologies were even made by some of his officer colleagues to Hanna. She was determined to get to the bottom of the incident which had so cruelly deprived her of a loving husband and Owen of a caring father. The Prime Minister had promised that Bowen-Colthurst would be court martialled. This case was heard at Richmond Barracks in Dublin in June and he was found guilty, but insane, of the murders of the three men. He was detained at Broadmoor and released 18 months later.

Hanna was not in any way satisfied nor were her father-in-law and uncle Eugene Sheehy. She now demanded a full public enquiry although the chances seemed remote. However, by her sheer tenacity, Hanna was able to secure a meeting with Prime Minister Asquith who offered her compensation. This she refused and continued to insist on the public enquiry. In the end she got her enquiry which started in August 1916 with the respected Sir John Simon presiding. The report came out in September but it did not satisfy Hanna. She relentlessly pursued the matter but with little further success. She refused offers of compensation although Mr Skeffington did insist on getting some for Owen. Hanna was not happy at the way her father-in-law had conducted himself during these testing days. And, to add insult to injury, Mr Skeffington had his son's body exhumed and reburied at Glasnevin cemetery. She always bore him a grudge for she had never consented to such action. She had not even been asked if she would consider the move. It left a sour taste in her mouth. She was now alone with Owen. Two of her other sisters were also widows by this stage leaving just Kathleen with her husband still alive.

Hanna takes her message to America

After the trauma of Francis's death and the fiasco of the public enquiry, Hanna received an invitation to visit America. The United States were not yet in the war and it seemed an ideal opportunity for Hanna to go and do what she could to keep them out of the conflict. But it was difficult to get out of Ireland. However, with the help of her friends, she was able to leave without the necessary documents and even travelled under a false name. She took Owen with her. She was now 40 years old and Owen eight. When they arrived in New York Hanna made immediate arrangements to board out her son with an American family and then to enrol him at a Montesorri school in Santa Barbara, California. He would be in safe hands and would receive a good education. This allowed Hanna to proceed with her tour.

She travelled from city to city delivering her message to receptive audiences. Her style was straightforward and she enjoyed putting her story over. She had hoped to influence the Americans but, unfortunately for her, the United States entered the war when she was there. Whilst there were many groups of people who were anxious to hear her, there were those who opposed her and got her speeches censored. All in all the tour did go well and Hanna Sheehy Skeffington was considered to have been a great hit with those who eagerly waited to hear what she had to say. The culmination of her tour was the surprise audience she had with President Wilson especially when what she had to say ran totally contrary to his thinking.

Mother and son returned home in June 1918. During their absence more significant changes had occurred in her family. Her mother and uncle Eugene had died but, on a happier note, her sister, Kathleen, had given birth to her son, Conor Cruise O'Brien. Life had changed in Ireland. The war was coming to a close; many young Irishmen had died in the Allied cause but yet the British were still in charge in Dublin. She was pleased to note that the Irish Women's Franchise League was still going strong; the *Irish Citizen* continued to be published and at last women over 30 had the vote. Hanna felt vindicated that her strenuous actions had borne some fruit although there was still a long way to go.

Return to Ireland

Hanna had been granted a passport to return to Britain as far as Liverpool but she was not permitted to cross the Irish Sea to Dublin. However her high profile brought a number of influential MPs to her aid and the British government, much embarrassed, allowed her to come home. One of the first people she went to see was Michael Collins who had been running a fund raising campaign and she was able to hand over to him the useful financial contributions which she had gathered whilst on her American tour. There were few people of importance that Hanna did not know.

But almost immediately upon her return Hanna was again arrested as persona non grata in the country and sent to the Bridewell. As ever she started a hunger strike which this time rather backfired on her. She was released only to be removed, not to her home, but to Holloway Prison in London. At that time in Holloway there were other Irish women whom she knew well, Constance Markievicz, Maud Gonne and Kathleen Clarke, the widow of the executed Tom Clarke. Having, as it were, caught up with her friends' news, Hanna commenced yet another hunger strike and was released to a London hotel and finally allowed to go back to Dublin.

She used a slightly more cautious approach this time and went back to her paper, resuming the editorship after a long absence. That the paper was still in circulation greatly satisfied her. Her words in the next editions reiterated her demand for equal women's rights and also continued to condemn the British and American franchise movements which had lapsed during the war rather than, like her own organisation, keeping up a relentless campaign of vitriol against the government. With the war eventually over in November 1918, there was the prospect of a general election. Hanna joined the Thomas MacDonagh Sinn Fein club and was chosen to contest the Dublin Harbour division in the election. But this was not for Hanna and she declined the offer. She did however become a member of the Sinn Fein executive and she was now being invited to address various clubs throughout the country. On reflection it hardly mattered that she did not stand in the election. The Sinn Feiners won 73 seats and caused the utter decimation of the Irish Parliamentary Party which was reduced from around 80 seats to just six.

During the War of Independence, often known as the Black and Tan war, Hanna continued to be in demand as a speaker. She was elected as a Dublin county councillor in 1920 which gave her an added platform to promote her views which remained strident and uncompromising. Her public speaking became renowned which pleased her as she remembered the earlier days when she was not a confident orator. She interceded for young Kevin Barry in October 1920 but was unsuccessful in saving his life. He was executed on 1 November 1920 which was an unbelievably insensitive day for the British to carry out the sentence. It was All Saints' Day, a significant and important day in the church calendar.

Hanna became the Director of Organisation for Sinn Fein around this time too and used her vast administrative skills to reorganise many Sinn Fein clubs throughout the country. By the end of the Treaty talks in London in December when Collins and Griffith returned to Dublin having signed the document opposed by de Valera, Hanna took his side and along with the Irish Women's Franchise League stood up against it. Her militancy showed no sign of diminishing.

Hanna Sheehy Skeffington – outright Nationalist

Hanna had started her outspoken career as a feminist and suffragette. By 1920 she had become a true Nationalist. Her organisation's paper *Irish Citizen* had fallen by the wayside in 1920 after eight good years in publication. She had run a very creditable journal and had been successful in promoting the feminist causes through its pages. It was time for something different, but no less taxing and strenuous for a woman now well into her forties. By 1922 she had taken up yet another invitation to return to America and this time her lecture tour took her to twenty five of the United States. It was a profitable time for her Nationalist cause and she earned a great deal of money to bring back to Ireland for the Prisoners'

Dependents' Committee. In Ireland her friend, Maud Gonne, had formed a similar organisation for women – the Women's Prisoners' Defence League - and Hanna worked as hard as ever for them. It seemed that she was rarely at home spending most of her time giving talks, raising funds and encouraging people throughout the country to support her just causes.

Life in Dublin during the 1920s after the calamitous Civil War continued to be nothing less than a roller coaster ride for Hanna. She got involved with the protests outside the Abbey Theatre against Sean O'Casey's *The Plough and the Stars*. Like so many like-minded people she did not like the way that O'Casey had portrayed the Irish peasant and she would have shown her displeasure to the formidable Lady Augusta Gregory and the poet, WB Yeats, whose work for the renascent Irish theatre was legendary.

By 1926 she had been appointed to de Valera's new Fianna Fail party's executive although she broke with them the next year when the party decided to enter the Dail by getting round the signing of the oath by actually doing so. Hanna would have none of this and exited the party's ranks.

Once more significant family events bore down on Hanna. Her father-in-law, JB Skeffington, had died in 1919 and, although her relationship with him had never been brilliant, nonetheless she did miss him. In July 1927 her friend, Constance Markievicz, died in Dublin and she joined the throngs who followed the cortege to Glasnevin cemetery. She had also been named as one of the executors of Constance's meagre estate and she was to come into conflict from time to time with Constance's daughter, Maeve, over the provisions of the will. On Christmas Day 1927 her brother-in-law, Frank Cruise O'Brien, died leaving Kathleen with her 10 year old son, Conor. All the Sheehy sisters were now widows. On a brighter note, however, Owen had succeeded in gaining a scholarship to Trinity College and during his course he spent a year in Amiens, France, with the Denis family. He got to know one of their daughters, Andree, well and later married her.

Now Hanna became a constant traveller to various parts of Europe as a delegate for a number of organisations. When a high profile person was needed to fulfil these duties people looked no further than Hanna Sheehy Skeffington. In 1929 she attended the Women's International League of Peace and Freedom in Prague and on her return home met up with another friend, James Joyce. The next year, 1930, she was off to Leningrad and Moscow as a delegate of the Friends of Soviet Russia. She had taken a keen interest in Russia in recent times and found this experience invaluable and exciting for she felt herself very much attuned to communism. Her friends, Maud Gonne and Charlotte Despard, were at this conference as well. It was clear to see that these three Irishwomen were enthusiasts for whatever cause seemed uppermost in people's minds at any particular period.

Although Hanna did break with Eamon de Valera in 1927, she was still sympathetic to the Fianna Fail cause and continued to write articles for their newspaper *An Phoblacht*. She even became its assistant editor and, like her previous work with papers, she made a success of this venture too. She remained cautiously close to de Valera after he led them to power in 1932.

Hanna's twilight years

Family matters, of course, continued to impinge upon her life. Her father, David, died in 1932. He had had a wonderfully full life and had greatly influenced his children's lives with his love of Irish history. Hanna, too, had benefited from her father's zest for life, and in great measure. Her 42 year old widowed sister, Margaret, the mother of four children, had started a relationship with the 21 year old, Michael Brady, and soon had two children by him. They had left to live in Montreal, Canada, leaving three of her children with their Culhane relations. What Hanna thought of these events can only be speculated upon but she did go to visit Margaret during a further tour to north America.

Early in 1933, Hanna entered Northern Ireland to speak on one of her platforms. But she had been banned from entering the northern state and was promptly arrested and imprisoned in Armagh Jail for one month. She was still showing her determination, and perhaps her pig-headedness, by putting herself in such a position. She would have known what the consequences would be and yet she took the chance and paid the price.

It was during 1934 that she did return to America and Canada and undertook yet another successful lecture tour. One year later, in 1935, Owen married Andree Denis. Owen's health was never good and he suffered from various illnesses. He spent time in a Swiss sanatorium in 1937 and Hanna visited him there before heading out, yet again, for America. On her return this time further sadness struck her family. Kathleen O'Brien died and then Margaret's second husband, Michael, also died.

By 1939 with the Second World War now in full swing Hanna did some broadcasting, which she liked, and took time to set out her memoirs. She started to reduce her hectic commitments and lead a calmer lifestyle. Her own health was fairly poor for she suffered from a weak heart and blood pressure. She kept up her interest in teaching by giving classes in history, German and French at the Dublin Technical Institute. She even stood as an Independent in the 1943 Irish General election but failed to be elected.

Her first grandchild was born in 1945 and the next year she finally succumbed to her poor health. Hanna Sheehy Skeffington died on 20 April 1946 aged 68.

She left an indelible mark on Irish society; she vigorously fought for her causes and, due to her vibrant tenacity, women's rights were improved probably sooner than they would have been had it not been for her and her organisations. However it is true, and sad, to say that, like most women who fought and campaigned to improve the lot of women during those turbulent years of the early twentieth century, her contributions have been largely forgotten and even written out of Ireland's history.

Suggested reading
1. Levenson, Leah, *With Wooden Sword – a Portrait of Francis Sheehy-Skeffington, Militant Pacifist*, Boston 1983.
2. Levenson, Leah and Natterstad, Jerry H., *Hanna Sheehy-Skeffington – Irish Feminist*, Syracuse, USA, 1986.
3. Ward, Margaret, *Hanna Sheehy Skeffington – a Life*, Cork, 1997.

Edith Londonderry

Cosmopolitan Campaigner

Edith Helen Chaplin was born into the ranks of the nobility on 3 December 1878. She was the second of three children, two daughters and a son, of Henry Chaplin and his wife, Florence, who was a Levenson-Gower, the daughter of the third Duke of Sutherland. Lady Florence's childhood home was the enormous and romantic Dunrobin Castle in the north of Scotland. Edith's siblings were Eric, born in 1877 and Florence, born in 1881.

Her father, Henry, born in 1840, was the archetypal English gentleman and a keen horseman and huntsman. By the age of 19, however, both his parents were dead but he had been fortunate enough to inherit a considerable amount of land from one of his uncles. Henry was a popular young man although he tended to be extravagant and a spendthrift. He took to politics in his 20s and was elected Conservative MP for Sleaford in Lincolnshire in 1868. He married Lady Florence on 15 November 1876. He was also a great friend of his wife's brother, the heir to the Duke of Sutherland. But wealth and position in life did not favour Henry and Florence. Not long after the birth of their third child, Florence, Lady Florence became ill and died, leaving Henry a widower with three children after just five years of marriage. He was so devastated by the early and tragic death of his young wife that he never remarried. Neither did he take full parental responsibility for his offspring. The little Chaplins were brought up by their aunt Millie, the wife of the Marquis of Stafford, the Duke of Sutherland's heir and the friend of Henry. Millie and the marquis had a family of their own but were entirely happy to pour their love and affection on the three Chaplin children. Admittedly there were lots of staff and servants at Dunrobin to assist yet it was a big responsibility to add three more youngsters to their own. There was never any question of their father abandoning them, for he did come to visit, but the day to day care was not undertaken by him. He was largely absent throughout their formative years although Edith and her siblings always kept close contact with her father and loved him dearly.

During her childhood Edith spent lots of time both at Dunrobin and also at the Sutherland's home, Stafford House, near Buckingham Palace in London. She had, in today's parlance, an idyllic childhood learning to ride and care for horses and participating in the activities of the gentry. In 1892, when Edith was 13, her grandfather, the Duke, died and her uncle, the Marquis of Stafford, inherited the title. Back in Lincolnshire, however, Henry Chaplin had fallen on hard times. He was practically bankrupt and had to sell his home.

Young adulthood and marriage

Edith Chaplin was a beautiful and accomplished young woman. She was presented to Queen Victoria in the monarch's Diamond Jubilee year, 1897, and was already attracting the attentions of a most eligible young man, Charley, Viscount Castlereagh, the heir to the 6th Lord Londonderry. These men were, of course, the descendants of the famous Lord Castlereagh of Vienna Congress fame. They were also very rich with their money mainly coming from their coal mines. The

Londonderrys had a number of large houses throughout the country. Their chief mansion was Wynyard in county Durham, although they also had houses and land in Wales and Ireland, where Mount Stewart in county Down was the family seat.

Charley Londonderry had been born in the same year as Edith, on 13 May 1878. He was the second child, and first son, of his parents. His mother was the formidable Theresa who was known as London's finest hostess in the family's London home, Londonderry House, in fashionable Pall Mall. She was also reputed to have had an eye for the men and was rarely faithful to her husband. Her son, Charley, was to follow in his mother's rather unpredictable and capricious amorous footsteps. His father had been the Lord Lieutenant of Ireland from 1886 until 1889 and he was the first Irishman to hold this position. Charley attended school at Eton, then went to Sandhurst and eventually joined the army.

Charley and Edith became engaged in August 1899 and were married in St Peter's, Eaton Square in London on 28 November 1899. He was 21 and Edith just short of her 21st birthday. At the start of their married life they lived in a flat in Londonderry House under the watchful, and doubtless prying, eye of the Marchioness Theresa. They did, however, buy a small house at Oakham in Rutland which became something of a double-edged sword. It did mean that Edith was away from her powerful mother-in-law but it also meant that she was on her own a great deal of the time owing to Charley's repeated and lengthy absences from home as he pursued his amorous adventures. From this early stage of their marriage Edith had to get used to her husband's flights from home. She became depressed especially when it became clear that her husband was a notorious philanderer. From the day and hour of his marriage, and even before, Charley was unfaithful to Edith. She was soon to discover that Charley had had an affair with a beautiful actress called Fannie Ward who was seven years older than he was. To make matters worse she was pregnant at the time of the wedding and her child, Dorothe, was born in February 1900. To Edith's eternal credit she always forgave her husband for his indiscretions. Having married into the upper echelons of high society Edith had to swallow her pride and keep a stiff upper lip. Divorce in those days would have caused scandal and she did not want to be a party to such a public indignity.

By the end of 1902 and three years of marriage, Edith and Charley had two children, their daughter, Maureen, born on 6 December 1900 and their son and heir, Robin, born on 18 November 1902. The new King, Edward VII, was the boy's godfather. The couple then spent some months in India in 1903 in order to allow Edith to recover from a bout of pneumonia. It was a welcome relief for Edith whose health soon improved.

Charley's father was keen for his son to enter politics. Charley was not so enthusiastic about the idea but bent to his father's will and fought the seat of Maidstone in Kent. The Tories were put out of office after this January 1906 election but Charley, contrary to everyone's expectations, won the seat with a slim majority.

But Charley's philandering continued much to Edith's obvious distress. He had an affair with Consuelo, the alluring American Duchess of Westminster and, in 1912, fell for Eloise, the Countess of Ancaster who also was an American. She had four children of her own at the time. Edith bore Charley's infidelity with great fortitude trying to keep an even keel for her children's sake. By this time, they had two more children, two daughters, Margaret, born on 9 March 1910, and Helen, born on 8 July 1911.

Edith decided to pursue outside interests for the sake of her own sanity. She supported votes for women and joined the suffragist movement which sought change by constitutional means. She became a popular and gifted platform speaker although her stance was strongly opposed both by her father and by Theresa, her mother-in-law. This broke little ice with Edith who genuinely felt that the time had come to give women equal voting rights under the law. Back in Ireland the Home Rule crisis was reaching its climax. Charley's father was a firm supporter of Edward Carson and the anti Home Rule faction although Charley himself was more lukewarm in his support.

The war years and the 'Ark'
Both Charley and Edith took their places on behalf of the war effort. Charley had hoped to join his regiment in France but was frustrated in his ambition when he was appointed as ADC to Sir William Pulteney. He would much rather have been in the midst of battle as opposed to undertaking what he saw as being a nugatory desk bound job. Edith, however, was glad he was not in the trenches. With time on his hands Charley pursued a line he knew well. He started writing letters to Ettie, Lady Desborough, described as 'a tragic, but brilliant socialite'. He progressed then into a long-standing affair with this titled lady which only ended when the war was over. On the plus side, however, Charley was becoming interested in flying and aviation and was instrumental in helping to get the Royal Air Force, founded in 1918, off the ground. Flying was to become a passion for Charley in the years to come.

As far as Edith's contribution was concerned she enthusiastically involved herself in the Women's Volunteer Reserve to which organisation she was appointed Colonel in Chief. Soon she realised that this was not the place for her as she considered their members to be too militaristic. She then quickly formed the Women's Legion which carried out sterling work during the conflict by placing women in farm work to cover for the men who had been conscripted to the services. The women, under Edith's inspired leadership, performed a job second to none. For her services to the Legion and the war effort Edith was created a Dame of the British Empire at the end of the war.

In February 1915 Charley's father, the 6th marquis, died which meant not only that Charley was the new marquis but, more importantly in many ways, Theresa was no longer chatelaine and mistress of all she surveyed. There was a new marchioness, Edith, and the spotlight of necessity turned away from Theresa and fell upon Edith. Things were somewhat strained for a while although Edith quickly became as consummate a hostess as her mother-in-law had ever been.

In the months following her father-in-law's death, Edith had a brainwave which helped to keep her in the public eye and in the limelight. She had, of course, many influential friends, many of whom were engrossed in the serious work of ensuring an Allied victory in the war. So she started her 'Ark'. This was a group of her friends who were invited weekly to Edith's home to take time out for their hard work and pressure to find a little period of respite, time to meet friends and discuss the less weighty aspects of life. To each member Edith gave the name of a real or mythical beast. And so it was that she herself became Circe the Sorceress, Charley was the Cheetah, Winston Churchill the Warlock, Edward Carson the Eagle, Hazel Lavery the Hen and Sir John Lavery the Dory. They appreciated the fun and fellowship of the group and thanked Edith for the opportunity to take time out from the pressures of daily life.

Charley continued to be bored as an ADC but eventually he realised his ambition. After becoming second in command of his regiment's reserves for a period he got his wish to go into the muddy trenches in early 1916. He met Edith on several occasions in France for she was often there in her capacity as leader of her Women's Legion.

By mid 1916 Charley was back home undertaking his work as an MP. The ill fated convention which took place in Dublin from the summer of 1917 until the spring of 1918 was the brainchild of Prime Minister, David Lloyd George, by way of trying to find a solution, by peaceful means, to the intractable problems of Ireland. Charley was asked to be the secretary for the Ulster Unionists who only reluctantly took part in what became no more than a talking shop. Lloyd George had successfully defused the situation, at least for a time. Charley did not enjoy his posting but had no option but carry out his responsibilities. The convention, needless to say, was a complete failure and kept people like Charley from undertaking their duties on the battlefield.

Back home Edith was pleased when she heard that her aging father had been given a peerage as Viscount Chaplin. At last the war ended in November 1918. Sorrow and heartbreak had affected almost every family in the land. Edith and Charley had survived but many of their friends and relations had lost sons and heirs. Even two of Lady Desborough's sons had been killed in the trenches.

The inter-war years

Edith's hard work during the war had not only resulted in her being gazetted a Dame of the British Empire but she was pleased that her suffrage campaign had also brought the vote to women, at least to those over 30. It had been a hard fought campaign and much of the credit was owed to Edith Londonderry. The women's first opportunity to exercise the franchise came at the so-called 'khaki' election in the December of 1918. Edith was now universally well known not only in elevated circles but also amongst the general population.

On 15 March 1919 the indomitable and indefatigable Theresa died aged 62. For Edith this meant that her mother-in-law was no longer looking over her shoulder and so she could continue to impress her many guests at her soirees and balls at Londonderry House. These spectacular gatherings were also helping the socially wayward Charley as he progressed in his political career. He was now the Under Secretary for Air and, although not a cabinet post, it still meant a big promotion for him which allowed him to advance the needs and opportunities for the RAF. However he still continued to be absent from his home for long periods leaving Edith feeling guilty and needlessly blaming herself for Charley's indiscretions.

On 25 March 1921 Edith's youngest child, another daughter Mairi, was born at Mount Stewart. It had been over twenty years since their first child was born and, by that time, Maureen was married and actually gave birth to her first child just five months after her youngest sister was born.

By now Edith had had enough of her English homes. She decided to make Mount Stewart her main residence. During their ownership of this fine house on the beautiful Ards peninsula, the Londonderry family had let it go to rack and ruin. Edith made it her aim to restore it to its former glory and in this she unquestionably succeeded. She was indeed fortunate to be able to enlist the help of a number of local men who had been discharged from the army after the war and who were unemployed. With their assistance Edith transformed the glorious gardens of this stately home. She created all sorts of lovely ponds, flower beds and shrubberies which are still admired to this day. Close to the house she also set out a special patio area which contained statues of the various beasts from her 'Ark'. Edith was really content in her endeavours at Mount Stewart and she was at peace with herself.

In the year of Mairi's birth, 1921, came the partition of Ireland with the new Province of Northern Ireland set up alongside the Irish Free State. The newly formed government of Northern Ireland under Prime Minister, Sir James Craig, needed politicians of calibre. They were hard to find. Craig approached Charley to join his cabinet as Minister for Education and leader of the Senate. Charley was in two minds whether or not to accept what could well become a poisoned chalice. However he had been unsuccessful in his attempt to become the Viceroy of India and so he accepted the challenge in Northern Ireland. It was a difficult time for the new Ulster Prime Minister and especially for the landed families in Ireland. Immediately post partition came the Irish War of Independence and then the Civil War during which time countless of the stately homes of the Anglo Irish were burnt to the ground. Although things were better in the north eastern counties there were still a number of homes there destroyed by the IRA. Mount Stewart was attacked on at least one occasion but thankfully damage was limited. Their neighbour in the nearby village of Strangford, Lady de Ros, was not so lucky. Dragged out of her bed in her nightclothes she had to stand on her front lawn and watch her home, Old Court, go up in flames. It was a most stressful time particularly for the gentry families.

Charley worked hard as a minister in the government. He was, perhaps after Craig himself, the most experienced politician in Northern Ireland. He also was a most proficient Education Minister and in 1923 introduced an education act. However there was strenuous opposition from the clergy, both the Roman Catholics, which was predictable, but more so even from intransigent Protestants. Had the act gone through education in Northern Ireland would have been straightforward with every pupil in an area going to the same local school and their separate religious education needs seen to at the end of a school day in separate classrooms with their own clergy. That lesson completed the youngsters would have joined together again to make their way home. Sadly this was not to be and education remains to this day one of the ongoing problems facing each succeeding administration. After this, by early 1926, Charley resigned from the government and returned to England.

At the end of 1921 there were the so called 'Treaty' talks between the representatives of the British and the new Free State governments. Edith was slightly involved in this process. The Irish delegation met many of their sympathisers in London including John and Hazel Lavery. At their home Edith was present on occasions and there she met Michael Collins. Both Charley and Edith came to like and admire Collins, a position taken by a surprising number of British representatives. There exists a letter sent by Collins to Edith and there are those who would say that perhaps there was a certain bond being built up between them. There would hardly have been any sort of liaison but it shows what sort of personality the charismatic Collins was. The talks never pleased Craig and he never participated saying that partition was a reality and he had been put in charge of Northern Ireland and would brook no interference. Collins carried back a treaty much to the chagrin of his leader in Dublin, Eamon de Valera. The treaty held and Ireland was able to make progress.

Another chapter for Edith closed in 1923 when her father, Viscount Chaplin, died. She felt his death deeply but knew her life had to go on.

The Ramsey McDonald connection
Edith Londonderry and the Labour politician, Ramsey McDonald, became close friends at the beginning of the 1920s. To the general public they seemed such strange bedfellows although, for all his socialist credentials, he preferred the company of Tories and other prominent members of the aristocracy. His parliamentary colleagues disdained their leader's choice of companions but he was able to put his association with the gentry, especially the Londonderrys, to good use during the 1926 General Strike. He used his influence with Charley Londonderry to persuade him to keep his mines in the English coalfields open even if they were making

a loss. To be fair to Charley he was of a mind to be reasonable with his workers anyway understanding what privations they were suffering. In the general election of 1929 McDonald was again the Prime Minister although, on the minus side, Edith's son, Robin, lost his seat at Darlington.

Edith's and McDonald's friendship strengthened and he was delighted when Edith invited him to become a member of the 'Ark', being styled Ramsey the Ram. However in 1931 when he was the head of a national government, McDonald was expelled from the Labour Party. He came more and more to rely on Edith's consoling words and actions which led to many rumours that they were closer than just friends. His health deteriorated and he was often in hospital which happened to be close to Londonderry House. As Edith continued to visit him, McDonald became infatuated with her. Charley never seemed to bother about what was being said about Edith and her friendship with McDonald.

Flying was beginning to take a prominent place in the lives of Charley and, to a lesser degree, Edith. Charley owned a number of planes and they had a small airstrip at Mount Stewart. The family was soon to build, in 1934, the airport at Newtownards. At Mount Stewart members of the family also enjoyed sailing activities especially with the closeness of Strangford Lough. Edith took part in many of these pastimes but she never gained her pilot's licence.

In the years of the Depression Edith involved herself in further good works. A Personal Service League, which she set up with her titled friends to help clothe the unemployed, foundered but she did all she could to show her compassion and assisted when she could. In the meantime, Charley kept imploring the lacklustre government in London to pay more attention to what was happening in Europe with the Germans and Italians up to their tricks by building up their air forces and rearming at an alarming rate. This was to become Charley's crusade of the 1930s. He was determined to make those in government realise the dangers the country was in and to urge them to rearm. His pleas fell on deaf ears.

Charley continued to have affairs through his mid fifties. Edith continued to turn a blind eye. She knew her husband and his roving eye. In these years their children were marrying but, sadly, many of the unions were disapproved of or ended in divorce.

Ramsey McDonald resigned as Prime Minister in 1935 having become absentminded and rather unreliable. Both he and his son, Malcolm, lost their seats in the general election in November 1935 and, much to Charley's chagrin, Stanley Baldwin, McDonald's successor, sacked him from his government post.

The country was descending into chaos. The abdication crisis at the end of 1936 rather epitomised the lethargy and discontent of the nation. The Londonderrys totally disapproved of the new King's association with Mrs Wallis Simpson although they did sympathise with the King's plight in a letter to him wherein there was no mention whatsoever of Mrs Simpson.

Charley was depressed and anxious about the country's future especially when it looked certain that a conflict was likely to break out sooner rather than later.

The German contacts

Even although Charley had been Air Minister he still could not persuade, cajole or threaten his colleagues in cabinet into rearming more quickly. He could see that urgency was vital and could not believe the head in the sand attitude of the government. He decided to take matters into his own hands. He would go to Germany and beard the lion in his den. He would see if there was any chance of finding friends amongst Hitler's closest associates. There were those who now accused him of being a Nazi sympathiser. At all times Edith stood firmly behind her husband.

Immediately after attending the funeral of King George V in January 1936, Charley, accompanied by Edith and Mairi, set off for Berlin where they met Goering and Hitler to try to find out what they could. The Londonderrys were treated like royalty and even visited the Olympic Games then being held in Berlin. Upon return to London government ministers were somewhat displeased about Charley's visit to Germany but there were those who realised that what Charley did had been the right thing to do.

Back in London the German minister in the capital, the social climber Joachim Ribbentrop, who liked to style himself von Ribbentrop though he was not from an aristocratic background, got to know the Londonderrys. Neither Edith nor Charley could stand Ribbentrop but they knew they needed to keep him on side and even invited him to Mount Stewart as their guest. In the end any rapprochement between the British and the Germans was not to be and war broke out on 3 September 1939. Britain was still badly prepared and soon came to realise that much of what Lord Londonderry had said was perfectly correct. The 1938 visit by Chamberlain to Hitler returning with his 'piece of paper' was something which caught in the throats of both Edith and Charley.

Before the war even broke out there were sadnesses and changes in the Londonderry family circle. Ramsey McDonald died in 1937 aboard a liner which was taking him on a voyage to south America and Dorothe, Charley's illegitimate daughter, and her husband were killed in an air crash at Randolph Hearst's ranch in California. Their small children became Charley's wards.

In 1938 Edith wrote what might be described as an autobiographical memoir entitled *Retrospect*. It was a rather disappointing and incomplete record of her life thus far.

World War Two and beyond

When the war broke out Edith was already 60 years old and Charley just a little older. They both wanted to be busy so Edith tried to resuscitate her Women's Legion activities. She also got involved with the Red Cross and brought her expertise and drive to these undertakings. She continued to help as many people as she could. As far as Charley was concerned he felt that he had been vindicated when Britain had to come to terms with not having sufficient aircraft and armaments to prosecute the war. The Battle of Britain put untold pressure on the RAF and, had it not been for the raw courage of the young pilots, the war would surely have been lost almost as soon as it had begun. Had it not been for the inspired choice of Winston Churchill as the country's leader in 1940, the outcome of the conflict could have been so different.

At home there was yet more sadness mixed with some good news. Mairi married Viscount Bury in 1941 but Margaret's marriage had fallen apart. Worse and sadder news was to come when Maureen, aged only 41, was diagnosed with TB and, after a spirited battle against the disease, died in June 1942.

Charley's own health was giving rise to concern. Soon after the ending of hostilities he was injured in a glider accident and, by the end of 1947, he was having a number of minor strokes. Edith helped him through these hard times although she herself was poorly. Charley Londonderry died on 10 February 1949, aged 70, and was buried within the grounds of Mount Stewart in consecrated ground at the rear of the main garden in a special burial place called Tir N'an Og. He was succeeded as 8th marquis by Robin who himself died just six years later in 1955 aged only 52. Even his own wife had died before him in 1951 only having been the marchioness for barely two years. It was a sad and sombre time for Edith who had lost her husband, her only son and her eldest daughter in a relatively short space of time. She herself developed cancer in 1957 and, not long after her 80th birthday, Edith Helen, Marchioness of Londonderry, died on St George's day, 23 April 1959. She had left much to her family in particular and to the country in general. A worthy and kindly woman, Edith had helped to progress votes for women, she had given assistance to those who had needed it during two world wars and had been a loving mother and a patient and forgiving wife to a wayward husband. Her legacy lives on to all of us who visit her fine home on the Ards peninsula.

Suggested reading
1. De Courcy, Anne, *Circe – the Life of Edith, Marchioness of Londonderry*, London, 1992.
2. Hyde, H. Montgomery, *The Londonderrys – a Family Portrait*, London, 1979.
3. Kershaw, Ian, *Making Friends with Hitler – Lord Londonderry and Britain's Road to War*, London, 2004.

Hazel Lavery

Spirited Socialite

Edward Martyn and his wife Alice were wealthy Americans. Edward had been brought up in Massachusetts but had moved to Chicago, a city devastated by fire in 1871 but now becoming vibrant and revitalised once again. By the late 1870s he had made great progress in the firm of meat packers where he worked and it was at this time he met his future wife. At the time of their marriage Edward was 31 and his wife ten years younger. Edward was particularly proud of his Galway roots and instilled in his children a love of Ireland. A little unusually his was not a Catholic Irish American family but an Episcopalian one. Later in life Edward would contend that his Martyn family was related to the prominent Galway family, of Tullira castle in the county, but there did not appear to be any justification in the claim. Perhaps it was Edward's way of impressing his friends and neighbours.

On 14 March 1880, the Martyn's first child was born. This was a daughter to be called Ella until her parents saw her hazel eyes and changed their mind. She would be Hazel Martyn. Their second and last child, Dorothy, was born seven and a half years after Hazel in November 1887. This little girl was, in her short life, to be constantly in the shadow of her elder sister.

Edward continued to prosper, climbing the social ladder and becoming one of Chicago's wealthiest citizens. He moved from one beautiful house to another and travelled all over the United States and in Europe. As a child Hazel always looked forward to her father's return from his various trips so that she could learn all she could about the wonderful places he had visited and to be told all sorts of romantic stories of his adventures. She revelled in being the child of such a prominent person in that great city.

Hazel was never going to be sent to a local school. She was taught at home in the first instance by her mother and then attended a private school. Finally she was packed off to an upmarket Episcopal college in Wisconsin for her last years of learning. But like all young ladies of the upper class Hazel spent a term or two at a finishing school near New York and here she took an interest in music and painting. By age 17 Hazel Martyn was ready for the world. She was confident, popular and self-assured and looked forward to launching herself into the society world of Chicago. But as is so often the case there was a sting in the tail, an unexpected twist to confound plans so carefully laid.

In April 1897, Edward Martyn suddenly died aged barely 50. The family was heartbroken and disconsolate especially Hazel, then just 17. Her little sister was just 10 years old. Alice Martyn, who, for so long totally reliant on her sophisticated husband, found the transition to widowhood hard to bear. From then on, although left with plenty of money, her life started to fall apart. Hazel's life, on the contrary, moved relentlessly forward. With the lessons learnt at finishing school Hazel Martyn took her first steps into the world, a blossoming socialite. She attended balls, visited the great theatres of New York and, above all, kept in the public eye. Everyone was aware of this beautiful young woman and, although her name was not exactly on everybody's lips, at least her photograph was appearing regularly in the influential newspapers of the city.

Moving into adulthood and an unhappy marriage

At finishing school Hazel had taken a keen interest in painting and her teachers were greatly impressed by her progress. In 1898 she travelled to France where she had the good fortune to become immersed in the life of the impressionist painters. Although not much is known about her own early artistic works, she certainly had fallen on her feet by meeting artists whose names were so well known.

Back home Hazel fed off her new found publicity. With the help of her mother she organised an elaborate gathering at her home, almost reminiscent of a court presentation. It was reported in the local press that hundreds of guests had attended to view 'this astonishing beauty'. She was hailed as an artist of note and even held a number of exhibitions, although her mother still did not approve of her daughter's chosen vocation. Nonetheless Hazel's work was finding popularity in Chicago. She must have been talented for such a hard-headed sort of place as Chicago to approve so enthusiastically of her displays. She was now determined to perfect her painting skills so she returned to France, this time to Paris, to pursue her burgeoning career.

Her mother, however, was beginning to squander her inheritance and was obliged to sell her lovely home and go to live in a hotel suite. She even approached her late husband's firm to borrow money from them. Hazel may have been uncertain as to her mother's fate but she seemed sure of her own destiny.

In 1903 Hazel once more returned to France, to Beg-Meil on the Brittany coast which was another popular haven for the impressionist painters. And it was here that Hazel's life was to change irrevocably. There she met the accomplished Belfast born painter, John Lavery, and it was not long before each was captivated with the other. Hazel was then 23 years old and John 47. The age difference did not seem to matter. They enjoyed each other's company and Hazel learnt a great deal about painting from John. Hazel was flattered by John's attentions although, back in America, Alice Martyn had other ideas for her daughter. She may have been displeased at Hazel's chosen profession but she was even more horrified at her daughter's choice of companion. She was unimpressed by John Lavery regardless of his prominence in the field of art and she was of one mind to divert the course of Hazel's love towards someone she considered more suitable and eligible. Back in France Hazel was blissfully unaware of her mother's dastardly machinations. She had fallen in love with Lavery and thought him 'great, wise and solemn'. She knew of Eileen, the daughter of her already widowed John and it was not long before he had proposed marriage and a home in London for his lovely Hazel.

But problems were in store for Hazel. Her mother, who had arrived in Paris to see the situation first hand, refused to allow Hazel to go to London with John. She informed Hazel that she had a young man in mind who would marry her.

This was Ned Trudeau, a successful 30-year-old Chicago doctor, who was a great admirer of Hazel's and who relished the chance to offer his hand in marriage. Alice even brought the young man to Paris. Hazel, however, had different ideas. She disliked Ned and informed her mother accordingly. Alice ignored her daughter's entreaties and insisted that Hazel break off her relationship with John and return to Chicago to marry Ned. Hazel, knowing that she could not resist her mother, sorrowfully bade farewell to a discomfited and unhappy John. Alice Martyn had got her way. Her daughter would marry someone with 'prospects' and not an impecunious artist.

Hazel's wedding to Ned took place at the end of December 1903 in a very stylish ceremony at her own episcopal church in Chicago. From the outset Hazel was profoundly unhappy and yearned for John to whom she even wrote on her wedding day. She was bitter at her mother whom she felt had treated her most callously. However this was the day and age when even a rebellious daughter could not get her own way. The Trudeaus moved into a fashionable apartment in New York where Ted was serenely content. His new wife, on the contrary, was restless and miserable.

Ned continued his work at the hospital where he practised which was, at that time, filled with very overcrowded wards. As a consequence he contracted pneumonia but seemed to be on the way to recovery. He came home one day in early May 1904 and suddenly dropped dead on the floor. He was buried a few days later after only five months of marriage. Thus, by this unexpected turn of fate, Hazel was released from a bond which she had never wanted. But she soon discovered that she was not yet free. She discovered that she was pregnant and in October gave birth to a daughter, Alice. She was pleased that her child was well after a difficult delivery but knew she now had responsibilities with which she had not reckoned.

Another marriage, this time a very happy one

The following summer Hazel travelled, with her mother and baby, to Malvern Wells in Worcestershire in England. Hazel continued to enjoy painting and was once more corresponding with John. He left his artists' enclave in Brittany and came to see Hazel where he painted one of his best known works of Hazel entitled *Dame en Noir*. But the spectre of Mrs Martyn still loomed over the love affair. She had not changed her mind and forbade Hazel from seeing John. She even enforced a six month separation and insisted on no letters or meetings. Once more Hazel had no alternative but to conform. It is likely that money was involved and her mother held the purse strings. Not even Hazel could find a way around these problems and, as a consequence, became severely depressed. Her world appeared to be falling apart.

A visit to Italy was arranged and this seemed to lift the doom and gloom pervading Hazel's life. Thankfully her health improved although there still was no correspondence between John and herself. Whilst the Martyns were visiting Rome, Hazel, as ever the attractive and alluring young woman, met another man. This was a 28-year-old American, Len Thomas. Their romance blossomed and Hazel wrote to John to inform him of her new beau. John tried to come to Rome to reason with Hazel but she forbade a visit. Arrangements were speedily being made back in America for the wedding when, as quickly as he had appeared, Len vanished into thin air. The vivacious Hazel had been unceremoniously jilted. Nothing more was heard of Len except some unwelcome rumours and, of course, there was no marriage. Hazel was now in a dilemma and, feeling thoroughly humiliated and ashamed, wrote to John fully expecting him to roundly rebuff her. Imagine her surprise and relief when he replied saying he would forgive his wayward Hazel.

The course of their love still did not run smoothly. Correspondence started once more but Hazel was back in Chicago looking after her sick mother, her hypochondriac sister, her ailing grandparents and, naturally enough, her little daughter, now aged three. This would have been a most trying time for Hazel but her biographers have found none of the letters between John and Hazel. In all likelihood they were destroyed. This must have been the worst and most difficult time for Hazel.

But the dreariness eventually lifted. In the spring of 1909 the entire Martyn family entourage, with the exception of her grandfather who had died the previous year, arrived in London and travelled once more to Paris. Mrs Martyn's view of John Lavery as a prospective son-in-law had still not changed. There was some contact between John and Hazel but nothing approaching a full reconciliation. Once more the family repaired to London in anticipation of travelling back to the States. But once more destiny intervened. Whilst in London, in June 1909, Mrs Martyn developed appendicitis and died aged just 51. Hazel returned to Chicago with her mother's remains where the funeral took place. Sad though she was at her mother's death, Hazel was free at last.

John Lavery and Hazel Trudeau married in that great Catholic church in London, Brompton Oratory, on 22 July 1909 just five weeks after her mother's demise. The two children of their first marriages, Eileen, John's by his first wife, and Alice, Hazel's child by Ned, were both delighted at their respective parents' new union. John had always loved little Alice and Eileen, who actually only met Hazel at the wedding, was on good terms with Hazel throughout their lives. She returned for a while to her American home to settle her mother's affairs and make the best care arrangements she could for her ailing sister.

Hazel took up residence as Mrs John Lavery in the beautiful 5 Cromwell Place in fashionable South Kensington. Hazel had, at long last, literally 'come home'. From this time onwards she was to become the consummate hostess; the society wife and, in course of time, the meeter and greeter and the fixer and politicker amongst the great and the good in England and in Ireland. She had set down her roots and would soon become London's best-known society icon.

John Lavery – artist extraordinaire
By the time of his marriage to Hazel John Lavery had already established himself in the art world. He had been born in Belfast in 1856 and had studied painting in Glasgow and then in Paris at the Academie Julian. He became a portrait painter of great renown and undertook many commissions throughout the British Isles. During his long life he painted members of the Royal family and almost every scion of the ascendancy throughout the country. As his life progressed he undertook war commissions during World War One and got involved in painting all the celebrities of the conflict between Great Britain and Ireland in the first two decades of the 20th century. But it was the number of portraits which he completed of his beautiful wife which never fails to impress. It is estimated that he captured Hazel in oils on more than 400 occasions and these works adorn the art galleries of the world to this very day.

The story continues
Hazel was now mixing with many of the most famous people in the land. The Prime Minister, Herbert Asquith, was a friend and a regular visitor to the Lavery home. It was a popular venue especially when Hazel's renowned fancy dress balls were in vogue. It was de rigueur to attend at Hazel's pleasure at her salons. In the midst of all this socialising, however, further family matters resurfaced on the other side of the Atlantic. Her sister, Dorothy, was becoming increasingly ill and she was not caring for herself. So, in 1911, Hazel and John, on his first visit to America, sailed for her childhood home to try to resolve the difficulties there with her sister. Dorothy travelled back to London with John and Hazel but she did not like the English capital. She soon returned home there to die late in 1911. Hazel was seen, by some of the American press, as a bête noir accusing her of not taking enough care of her sister. This reproof seemed rather harsh but she was able to live through the unkind criticism with her head held high. Even against this difficult backdrop, John had enjoyed the States and had been able to attract a number of commissions which were to become a lucrative source of income over the years to come.

Life in London suited Hazel very much. She was the centre of attraction whether at an event at her own home or in those of her friends. This type of frivolous company was not altogether welcome as far as John was concerned. He was essentially a private person and all these extravagant events made him feel rather uneasy. But he continued to accompany his wife as he saw it his duty to do so. And anyway everyone wanted to be painted not by John Lavery, but by Hazel Lavery's husband.

For a number of years before his marriage to Hazel, John had spent time painting and enjoying life in Morocco. Here he owned a house near Tangier and Hazel made her first visit to north Africa in the year she was married, 1909. As a very gregarious person Hazel was not too keen on the isolation and solitude of that country. She did of course make many friends but preferred her regular trips to the

British embassy where she could fraternise with what she saw as more civilised company. However little Alice loved the place making her visits there one of the highlights of her year. By 1914, however, the Laverys had given up their home in Morocco. Hazel's love of the high life in London had triumphed over the loneliness of north Africa.

Back in London Hazel resumed where she had left off. Her flamboyant parties continued and many of her visitors insisted on being painted by John, not in his studio, but in Hazel's house. The society men in the city now took a fancy to the lovely artist's wife. Men like Sir Shane Leslie, a relative of Winston Churchill's, and the restlessly flirtatious Charley, Lord Londonderry, the husband of Edith of Mount Stewart, county Down, fame, became captivated with Hazel. Charley Londonderry, who had more than his fair share of paramours throughout his life, in fact became infatuated with her. John Lavery reacted to the attentions and flirtations of these various men to his lovely wife mostly by taking it all in good humour. He realised that Hazel was no less than a stunning beauty and that it seemed almost natural for men with roving eyes to be attracted to her. As the years of their marriage progressed, however, John was to feel ever more uncomfortable. One advantage, of course, was that valuable commissions were ever forthcoming from those who had an eye for Hazel.

At the outbreak of the First World War, the Laverys were visiting Dublin. They hurried back to London where they saw the changes caused by the hostilities. John, although he was by now 58, joined the Artists' Rifles but was declared unfit for combat. The great friend of John and Hazel, Lady Edith Londonderry, had set up her 'Ark' which gave an opportunity for a group of friends to gather regularly in social surroundings to take their minds off the war. It was a most successful organisation with each of the famous members being given a name from mythology as a pseudonym. Hazel was known as the Hen and John the Dory. Edith herself was Circe and her husband, Charley, was known as the Cheetah. Not to be outdone Hazel invited many of her friends to 5 Cromwell Place for a bite of lunch and conversation. Both groups proved useful in diverting minds, if only temporarily, from the other more serious matters in hand. And it was during these gatherings that a friendship between John and Hazel and Winston and Clementine Churchill blossomed. It was even said that John gave Winston a few hints in the art of painting – from one artist to another.

During the war Hazel and John opened their home to raise funds for various war charities. As ever these events boosted morale amongst the fighting forces and Hazel's penchant for drama led to the performance of many tableaux vivants and plays performed not only at 5 Cromwell Place but also in the homes of her socialite friends. They remained popular throughout the conflict and brought in a great deal of money for many worthy and needy causes. John was appointed an official war artist but he was unable to fully fulfil his role in the battlefield owing to a car accident during a Zeppelin bombing raid over London. Both John and Hazel were injured causing distress to both of them and a nervous breakdown for Hazel. However both recovered to continue their good works. John was able to resume his official duties by painting forces returning home from the western front. For his services to the nation, he was knighted in the New Year's Honours List in 1918. Hazel was naturally pleased – for her husband of course but also because she would from now on become Lady Lavery – a title which she considered commensurate with her position in London society.

Ireland – and Hazel

Hazel's father, Edward, was descended from Galway stock and he had encouraged his daughter to be proud of her Irish heritage. But it was 1913 before Hazel, by then 33 years old, set foot on Irish soil. John and she visited Killarney that year, an outing which was repeated the following year. She was now beginning to think what her stance should be on the subject of Ireland's demand for independence from Great Britain. Both the Laverys were in favour of Home Rule for Ireland and had been pleased when, after many years of disputes and uncertainties, a Home Rule bill had finally been passed in 1914. But by this time the Great War had erupted and Ireland was once more put on the back burner.

The seminal event of the war, for Ireland at any rate, was the outbreak of the Easter Rising in April 1916. John and Hazel were as shocked as the rest of the population at the audacity of the event. It failed militarily, of course, but within five short years most of the country was independent. The Laverys were sympathetic to the Irish cause; they were against the mass internments and the executions after the Rising and they even attended the trial of Sir Roger Casement which took place in August 1916. One of John's finest and best-known paintings was of the court scene during the trial entitled *The Court of Criminal Appeal, London, 1916*. Whilst they abhorred the sentence of death imposed on Casement, both Hazel and John did their best to ride both political horses at the same time by condemning the execution but yet keeping in with the 'Castle set' – the British administration at Dublin Castle. They even continued to accept invitations to balls at the Castle. When the war finished and the general election of December 1918 returned over 70 'Sinn Feiners' to Westminster (seats which they never took) they more publicly damned the British. They now supported the embryonic, but still illegal, local Irish parliament called the Dail, which had been set up in January 1919.

During the dangerous days of the War of Independence in 1920 John and Hazel travelled frequently to Ireland and the major reason for this was the sudden upsurge in prospective commissions for the Irish leaders, on both sides of the divide, to be painted by the artist of the moment, Sir John Lavery. Many of the men who rose to prominence, Carson, de Valera and Collins were the subjects of Lavery portraits. These studies remain, to this day, as some of Lavery's best canvasses. In that same year, Hazel renounced her anglican background and converted to catholicism. She now felt more at home as an Irishwoman. Some said she even cultivated an Irish accent of sorts such was her degree of total immersion in her Irish ancestry. But she still could not convince Edward Martyn in Tullira that she was his cousin. She was not.

In the midst of the Treaty talks

During 1921 two series of talks were instigated to try to bring, once and for all, a resolution to the Irish question. In August Eamon de Valera came to London to talk to David Lloyd George – talks which were completely abortive and which simply turned out to be a talking shop between the Irish leader and the British Prime Minister. A further attempt was made in October. Eamon de Valera took what was to be a fateful step in Irish/British relations by sending a team of five plenipotentiaries led by Arthur Griffith and Michael Collins to treat with the strong British team led by Lloyd George and Lord Birkenhead. After six weeks it looked as if these talks would fail (which evidently pleased de Valera who remained firmly ensconced in Dublin). But the Irish did make peace with the British and signed an agreement which, though clearly not entirely satisfactory, did give them hope for the future, and a start to achieving their full demands in due course. De Valera and his hardliners in Dublin eventually lost the struggle and Griffith and Collins felt prepared to proceed with a local Irish administration.

Hazel Lavery was a small piece in Ireland's complicated jigsaw. But in the end she proved to be quite a significant piece and this is how it worked out. Firstly the Laverys understood the importance of these talks for the future of Ireland. They opened their home at 5 Cromwell Place to the Irish delegates as a refuge from the cut and thrust of the talks. At the same time John undertook preliminary sketches of a number of them. The Irish, however, were suspicious of the motives of the Laverys whom they considered to be spies for the British. But it was none other than Michael Collins himself who convinced his sceptical colleagues that their intentions were honourable and that they really wanted to do all they could to assist the Irish delegation. Collins himself was one of the Irishmen whose portrait John painted.

A rumour emerged that Hazel and Collins were having an affair and that she was over-influencing him to sign the Treaty. Whether or not this was the case, and the weight of evidence suggests that it was true, hardly matters at this distance in time. It is true that Hazel's persuasiveness was evident and that she did influence, in some small way perhaps, the positive outcome of the talks. There was much correspondence between Collins and Hazel but it was destroyed quickly afterwards. Hazel, this quasi-Irishwoman with her wealthy American background, seems to have been able to help to shape the future for Ireland. This may be hard to believe but, on reflection, her tenacity and closeness to Michael Collins were of great import. She was even able to keep in with the British authorities as well for she regularly wrote to Churchill gleaning what information she could. This she then passed to Collins to keep him in the picture. Regardless of what one may think of Hazel Lavery, her presence at this time did have a marked authority on both sides of the conflict. In the end the plenipotentiaries had their way. De Valera walked out of the Dail when his views had been rejected after lengthy debates leaving the way forward to be directed by Griffith and Collins. The real tragedy for Ireland was their sudden and unexpected deaths, one by natural causes and the other at the hand of an assassin, in August 1922.This left yet another chasm for Ireland to leap across during those early days of the Free State just as the Civil War was taking hold.

As the Civil War erupted at the end of June 1922, Irish politicians started to distance themselves from Hazel who considered her attachment to Michael Collins to be unsafe. And then, having taken up the army command as Commander-in-Chief of the Free State forces, Collins was killed at Beal na mBlath in county Cork on 22 August. Hazel was inconsolable since she had been seeing Collins nearly every day in the run up to his untimely death. She made up her mind to wear widow's weeds and was only dissuaded from doing so by wiser counsel. Nonetheless she was prominent at the requiem mass in Dublin and the subsequent funeral to Glasnevin cemetery. John had been immediately commissioned to paint Collins in his coffin at the lying-in-state and this became one of his greatest and best-known works which hangs to this day in the Hugh Lane Gallery in Dublin. It took Hazel a very long time to get over Collins' death. She carried about with her poems and letters which they had sent to one another. She visited his grave for weeks on end and talked about him incessantly to everyone she met. Her friends soon tired of hearing about Hazel's beloved Michael.

It is certain that John was very much aware of his wife's infatuation with Collins and, in all probability, knew of the possible intimacies between them. But he kept his counsel and concentrated on his painting which, for him, was his escape from the tittle-tattle which surely pervaded the salons of the rich and influential in Dublin. He continued to forgive his wayward wife but it was not long before he had to exonerate his wife yet again.

Hazel turns her affection in yet another direction
Soon after Hazel had got over the death of Michael Collins, she turned her attention to another prominent personality in Irish affairs. Following the demise of Griffith and Collins, the struggling Free State looked to two men to take over the mantle of running the government. WT Cosgrave and Kevin O'Higgins bravely stepped into the shoes of their dead comrades at a most difficult time for the country. In the midst of a most unwelcome and tragic Civil War, these men set forth on a path to keep the Free State's head above water. Kevin O'Higgins was a young man of terrific potential; he was a man of grim determination; he was a man of a strict and cold persona; he also was a man recently married with young children. He did not seem a likely paramour for the vivacious and beautiful Hazel Lavery. But not long after they met for the first time O'Higgins fell deeply in love with Hazel. He

started a long correspondence with her and no matter what state business he was pursuing, he still took time to send her love letters and poems. He was besotted with her. And, for Kevin and Hazel, the course of this true love certainly did not run smooth.

John and Hazel, accompanied by Alice, sailed for America where John had a great number of portrait commissions to fulfil. He was a most sought-after painter and had many places to visit to undertake his work. Hazel, still, one would assume, the reasonably dutiful wife, felt she had no alternative but to accompany her husband. But all the while she was missing O'Higgins and wrote constantly to him. He, in turn, was beside himself with anguish at this enforced separation. He wrote to her all the time. The visit lasted five months and it only can be imagined how overjoyed he was when the Laverys returned to Dublin.

Hazel now got involved in another of Ireland's continuing and most intractable problems – the future of the late Sir Hugh Lane's painting bequests. Lane was a nephew of the playwright and Abbey Theatre founder, Lady Augusta Gregory. He had finally decided to leave 39 iconic and valuable paintings to the Irish state. He had signed a codicil to his will during 1915 confirming his desire that these paintings should be returned from the National Gallery in London and donated to Dublin. But, surprisingly for such a punctilious man, he had omitted to have the will witnessed. And then he was drowned aboard the liner *Lusitania* which was torpedoed off the county Cork coast by German U-boats in September 1915. The difficulties surrounding these paintings have been the subject of continuing acrimonious debate ever since. Hazel, however, felt she could assist Lady Gregory and she set to with her usual determination. Sadly nothing conclusive came of her work with Augusta Gregory but it showed another side of Hazel Lavery. Life could be other than simply being self-centred.

The liaison between Hazel and Kevin O'Higgins progressed regardless. In November 1926 John informed Hazel that he had to go back to America where yet more clients were clamouring to be the subject of a famous John Lavery portrait. Hazel packed her bags once more and joined her husband. She dreaded going for she knew how the separation would affect O'Higgins, but she went. This time they did not return until March 1927. Immediately Hazel and O'Higgins renewed their affections and sadly, by this time, he had left his wife and children which caused yet more scandal and tongue-wagging throughout the city.

And then, as could only happen in the troubled Ireland of those days, yet another tragedy struck. On his way to Sunday mass on 10 July 1927, Kevin O'Higgins was gunned down outside the church in Booterstown. There had been a rumour circulating that an attempt would soon be made on his life. Little did he think that this dastardly deed would be carried out then. Once more Hazel was inconsolable; once more a lover had come to a tragic end; and once more John looked on realising that his wife's infidelities had finally got to him. From now on he was determined to keep a tight leash on his audacious wife. Many people wrote letters of condolence to Hazel at the death of O'Higgins just as if he had been her husband. Soon afterwards the Laverys set off to holiday in Scotland before going back, yet again, to America where more lucrative work beckoned.

Settling down in the Free State

John Lavery continued to paint prolifically. His work was known throughout Britain, Ireland and America. He now wanted to donate up to thirty of his best works to the Free State but his offer was dealt with in an offhand manner and with an inordinate delay. Annoyed at the unnecessary procrastination, John turned his eyes north to the city of his birth, Belfast. When offered a number of Lavery paintings to adorn its city art galleries, the Northern Ireland capital's authorities jumped at the chance and welcomed the gift with open arms. And just to prove how grateful the city was, the good burghers of Belfast made Sir John Lavery a Freeman of the city. He was to be the first artist to receive the accolade, and the first Roman Catholic.

Back in Dublin rumours were circulating that John might be offered the post of Governor General. John may have been flattered but Hazel scoffed at the idea. However soon afterwards came an offer which, as they say, could not be refused. As the new Free State was making preparations for the issue of its own currency, the powers that be approached the Laverys with a view to using one of John's many portraits of Hazel as the image to be depicted on their banknotes. John reworked one of his 1909 pictures which he renamed *Killarney* and, by 1928, when the new notes were eventually issued, it was the face of *Erin* or Hazel Lavery which adorned the currency. The choice of her face for the notes was not universally popular but the authorities stuck to their guns. It was Hazel's face that was handled by thousands of Irish men and women each day as they reached into the handbags and wallets to pay for goods in shops throughout the length and breadth of the Free State.

During 1928 the Laverys travelled to Northern Ireland to visit the Londonderrys at their county Down home on the lovely Ards peninsula, Mount Stewart. Hazel particularly liked Edith, the marchioness, and as they walked through the magnificent gardens on the estate, one wonders how much the two ladies discussed Edith's wayward husband's former attraction to Hazel and, strange though it may seem, both of their own attractions for the handsome Michael Collins. It had been said at a time that there might even have been a fascination between the wealthy socialite Edith and the rebel leader Collins. When Hazel was asked if she had liked the north she replied in the negative. The 'Black North' held no magnetism to the feisty Hazel.

Hazel, despite her leanings towards the new Free State, was still ambivalent about the country's motives. From time to time she was invited to functions at the former Vice Regal Lodge but was not impressed when they played the *Soldier's Song*. She also had contacts with the great and the good in British high society and when she had a cause to pursue Hazel Lavery could still pull strings and arrange audiences with Prime Ministers and members of the Cabinet.

There were developments too in their family life. Hazel's daughter became engaged to a Kilkenny man, Jack McEnery, in 1929. Hazel, like her mother before her, was displeased at Alice's choice of husband. He hailed from rural Ireland and was 13 years older than she was. Hazel seemed to have forgotten that she herself had married a man 24 years her senior. The real reason was probably that she was not going to be able to arrange a society wedding for her only daughter. In the end Alice got her way and she and Jack had their wedding in France. Hazel did not, however, attend the nuptials at which John was pleased to give away his stepdaughter.

Back in London

Hazel continued to be the centre of attraction. She hosted many afternoon teas and lunches for her friends and loved to attend the opening nights at the West End theatres. She cultivated friendships and made the acquaintance of George Bernard Shaw. Her roving eye was ever on the lookout for new and interesting beaux and she was soon surrounded by young admirers such as Bob Boothby and Randolph Churchill who just adored her.

Once more the paths of Edith Londonderry and Hazel Lavery crossed. At Edith's 'Ark' meetings Hazel had met the Labour Party's Prime Minister, Ramsey MacDonald. Although he was a rather elderly gentleman, he was still most handsome and attractive to women. Hazel once more entered into a liaison of sorts and voluminous correspondence flowed freely between the pair. Edith Londonderry herself had had an infatuation with MacDonald. It always seemed incongruous that this Labour man had such an affinity towards society ladies but this is just the person he was. This clearly irritated his own political colleagues who were less than pleased that their leader should be surrounded by what they clearly thought were little better than parasites. But the friendship between Ramsey and Hazel lasted some time even during an enforced separation caused by John's illness in 1931 when he and Hazel went off to the French Riviera for his recuperation. Needless to say many letters were written between Hazel and Ramsey during this episode of their lives. When they returned, John and Hazel made a visit to MacDonald's home in Scotland where, yet again, John had more painting commissions to complete. John continued to forgive his wife's unfaithfulness. He had learned to live with his capricious Hazel.

When Alice's first child, a son called Martyn, was born in 1931, Hazel's dislike for Jack seemed to dissipate and the family drew closer once again. Hazel herself, by now just over 50, was beginning to feel her age and took to painting her own face to keep up appearances. Melancholy and wistfulness were uppermost in her mind. Life seemed more and more empty and even desolate. Gone were the days of the society salons; gone were the days when every eye was concentrated on Hazel Lavery and gone was her ability to attract the attentions of the young men of the time. She would have been pleased, however, when the young writer, Evelyn Waugh, dedicated his first book to her, although when she looked across to Ireland to see Eamon de Valera take power in 1932, she felt great concern for the future of the country.

The last years of Hazel Lavery
By the end of 1933 Hazel had well passed her 53rd birthday. She had just had one of her wisdom teeth extracted and it was this seemingly innocuous ailment that was to lead to her final illness. She took to her bed. She was then diagnosed with myocarditis, an inflammation of the walls of the heart. She became so ill that nurses had to be brought into Cromwell Place to care for her. John's health, although he was by now in his upper seventies, was fair but he could not undertake the total care of his wife on his own. She was invited to a friend's house in Brighton in the hope of assisting her recovery but sadly she returned to London still very ill. She no longer saw visitors and she was alone with John.

Hazel Lavery died in her sleep on 3 January 1935 aged 54. Her funeral, attended by those who had known and loved her in her halcyon days, took place at Brompton Oratory. A further service was held later in Dublin to accommodate those friends who had been unable to travel to London. John died six years later in 1941 at the start of the Second World War, aged 84, and her daughter, Alice, lived on until 1991 when she died, aged 86, in county Meath.

With the passing of Hazel Lavery a bright light had been extinguished. She had contributed to so much in the life of her husband and in the eyes of so many influential people in Ireland's history in the early part of the 20th century. She was truly colourful, imaginative, manipulative, yet she had added spice and flavour to the dreary days surrounding the terrible years in Ireland's long and turbulent history. Future historians will mull over the life of this extraordinary lady. Many will say that her contribution was of little worth to the new Ireland, but my feeling is that the majority with any real appreciation of those tumultuous years will count important the contribution made by this beautiful and spirited woman.

Suggested reading
1. McCoole, Sinead, *Hazel – a Life of Lady Lavery 1880-1935*, Dublin, 1996.

Mary Bailey

Audacious Aviatrix

Mary Westenra was born on 1 December 1890 in London, the first of three children of Derrick (Derry), 5th Baron Rossmore, and Mittie, the daughter of Richard Naylor of Hooton Hall in Cheshire in England. The Rossmore's Irish seat was Rossmore Castle close to Monaghan town in one of Ulster's border counties in Ireland. The castle at Rossmore was an incredibly embellished and castellated mansion sitting amidst thousands of acres of land. Derry's father had, in fact, enlarged his family pile in the late 1850s. Derry was his parents' second son who would not have expected to inherit the estate and titles (for the Rossmore titles were both Irish and English). However, Derry's older brother died in a riding accident in 1874, leaving Derry the heir and custodian of Rossmore. He turned out to be a feckless and profligate country squire who more and more depended on his wife's wealth. Her father was an extremely rich banker who, at the time of his daughter's marriage, had frowned on Mittie's choice of husband. Mittie was soon writing cheques to cover Derry's various and ever increasing debts. Derry certainly fully appreciated his luck and good fortune at having married the daughter of 'the richest commoner in England'. Richard Naylor had amassed his fortune through banking enterprises and on horses, both breeding them and winning money on them.

And so Mary, later to be followed by her two brothers, William and Richard, was born into a family of privilege, troubled as it was, with constant parental disagreements over money. Regardless of her father's extravagant ways, Mary greatly loved him. Her relationship with her mother was much less warm and they never got on well throughout their lives.

The greater part of Mary's education took place at home as was the custom for the children of the gentry. She did spend one disastrous year at boarding school at Ascot and, such was her total loathing for the experience, she actually ran away from the school. Her parents did not return her but ensured that her education progressed at home through the excellent offices of two Russian sisters, Alma and Yelma Hemmerle. They proved not only good teachers but they also taught Mary French which was to stand her in good stead later on in life. Being at home also meant that Mary could pursue her favourite outdoor activity – horse riding. She became a most proficient horsewoman and was elected the master of the Monaghan Harriers when she was only 18 years old which was quite a coup for such a young woman. In this position she proved an excellent choice.

Mary did spend time in London for part of the year. It was de rigueur for titled families from Ireland to repair to their London houses for 'the season'. In 1909 Mary was presented at court to King Edward VII. Whilst this was undoubtedly an honour, Mary found life in the capital a total bore and wishing all the while that she was back at her beloved Rossmore. Returning home after her 'coming out' experience, Mary proceeded to buy herself a motor cycle which she used to good effect around the roads of county Monaghan, giving many of the locals, it must be said, plenty of unwanted scares as Miss Mary roared round their previously quiet highways and byways of the county and town. At the same time, just to further disturb the tranquil life of the countryside, Derry bought a motor car which was reputed to be the first such vehicular contraption in the area. He was a terrible driver without even having mastered the proper rudiments of driving the car. His chauffeur got him out of many a scrape. The locals may well have loved their squire and his feisty daughter, but they certainly could have done without their motoring shenanigans.

Mary's marriage and beyond

As a young woman Mary had plenty of friends amongst the landed classes in her part of Ireland. She was particularly close to Harold Alexander, a son of the Rossmore's neighbour, the earl of Caledon. Mary's mother had harboured thoughts that he would make a suitable husband for her tearaway daughter but it was not to be. Early in 1911, when she was still just 20 years old, Mary became engaged to be married to a 46 year old widower, Sir Abe Bailey. He had been previously married but, after just seven years, his wife had died. He had by then two children, a son, John, and a daughter, Cecil. It was never quite clear where Abe and Mary had met for he was a South African with great business interests in London. They may have been introduced at a race meeting but there seems to have been little by way of courtship. They married at Holy Trinity church in the city of London on 5 September 1911. The wedding was an elaborate and impressive affair with many fabulous and expensive presents. Immediately following the ceremony they came back to Monaghan for just a very few days where the local populace gave a reception and made many virtuous speeches for the newly weds. The Monaghan people were happy to see their much loved Miss Mary married but, like everyone else, they did wonder about her choice of husband.

Who, then, was Abe Bailey?

From his earliest years at home in South Africa Abe Bailey was a totally fearless child. He had run away from home when he was seven years old because he did not get on with his father. A family had taken him in and he proved to be a very self sufficient boy. He was at length restored to his home before being sent off to England to boarding school. He got a job on leaving school before eventually coming back to South Africa. Early on Abe had an eye for business. Having investigated the possibilities in the burgeoning gold mines, he turned his attention to becoming a claims broker and in this he prospered and, what is more, made many influential friends. Soon he was a wealthy man. He actually started to buy gold mines and amassed both money and influence. Before he was 30 he had become a Johannesburg town councillor and owned, amongst other things, a string of race horses. By now, in the 1890s, he had made the acquaintance of Cecil Rhodes whose influence and wealth extended throughout southern Africa. In 1894 he married Caroline Paddon who sadly died in 1902.

Abe had also been sent to jail after the ignominious and abortive Jameson raid and, in 1899, he fought in the Boer War. By the early days of the 20th century Abe and his friend and mentor, Cecil Rhodes, owned vast tracts of Africa. Abe had now fulfilled yet another of his ambitions when he was elected an MP in the Cape parliament. He was, at the same time, having a large house built at Muizenburg, north of Cape Town, for Rhodes. However Rhodes died in 1902 and so Abe went to live in the house. Abe had also inherited a farm of Rhodes' which was over a million acres. He was now the largest landowner in the country. Abe had always cultivated friendships with the Boers, especially men like General Louis Botha. Whilst a great supporter of the Crown and Empire, Abe nonetheless realised the importance of befriending the local population. He was able to use his influence for the good as he encouraged local young people to settle in places like the Transvaal. In 1911, at the time of his marriage, Abe was knighted by the King. He became a KCMG, an honour in the personal gift of the monarch. At the time of his marriage to Mary Westenra, Abe Bailey was a force to be reckoned with, not only in South Africa, but throughout the British Empire. His wealth was prodigious, a fact never lost on Derry Rossmore who had ensured that monies had to be 'made available' before he had consented to his daughter's marriage to this great South African magnate. He let it be known that, had a very generous settlement not been made, there would not have been a marriage.

South Africa – and a family

A few days after visiting Monaghan Abe and Mary set sail for Cape Town, a sea journey which lasted around three weeks. It was a cruise undertaken by both of the Baileys for the next number of years. They travelled, of course, in the height of luxury, and were feted by the crew and their fellow passengers as they looked forward to setting up their new home. They arrived at their home, Rust-en-Vrede ('rest and peace' in Afrikaans) by the middle of October 1911. Although much smaller than Rossmore Castle, their new villa was a more than comfortable house overlooking the bay north of Cape Town. Abe owned many other properties, of course, and was soon showing them off to his new wife. Mary soon began to fully appreciate her husband's great love and admiration for Cecil Rhodes.

It was not long before they had visitors from Ireland. Derry and Mary's two brothers, William and Richard, arrived in time for Christmas. Perhaps this was by way of a doting father inspecting the new surroundings of his beloved daughter. He seemed very satisfied as he and his sons went on further inspections of Abe's various holdings. They might not exactly have been awe-struck, but they were certainly pleased with what they saw.

Although Mary liked her new home she always preferred the northern hemisphere in England to the southern climes in South Africa so much favoured by her husband. In 1913 their first child, Mary Ellen, was born in England. None of the children were born in, or even visited, South Africa during their formative years.

The family was brought up in a rented house, 38 Bryanston Square in London, a house kept by the Baileys until 1930.

By now war clouds were looming and Abe suddenly decided to return to South Africa without even bidding farewell to his wife. There he joined up on the British side although he was, by then, well into his 50s. Mary then sailed for Cape Town leaving her little daughter in the charge of her parents in Monaghan. Abe certainly worked hard for the cause of the Empire during the duration of the Great War, even arranging for 20 sharpshooters to be sent to Europe. Sadly only six of these gallant men returned after the conflict. By the war's end, Abe was gazetted a baronet in the King's post war honours list.

Mary returned to England in 1915 and joined the women's section of the Royal Flying Corps, spending her time as a driver. By now she owned her own motor car. Towards the end of the war Mary gave birth to twins, Derrick and Ann, and the following year to another son, Jim. Her fifth and last child, Noreen, was born in 1921, the year of Ireland's partition when her home county of Monaghan became part of the Irish Free State, much to the chagrin of the landed gentry in that county as well as in Donegal and Cavan, the other two excluded Ulster counties. And it was in that same inauspicious year that Derry, Mary's father, died. Mary was heartbroken for she had lost her most precious connection with Rossmore and Ireland.

By the mid 1920s all her children were at boarding school, Abe was very often in South Africa and Mary Bailey had time on her hands. She then made the move which was radically to change her life. Whilst in the Royal Flying Corps at the beginning of the war, Mary had seen, and had envied, all the young men who flew aircraft. She wondered when women would be given the opportunity to emulate their male counterparts. She determined to effect a change. She decided to learn to fly believing firmly that anything men could do, women could do better.

Mary Bailey - aviatrix – and a journey of a lifetime
Now that Mary had little to occupy her time, she set about finding someone to teach her to fly. At the start she was secretive about her new-found hobby for she did not want to tell Abe who would have disapproved of her new ambition. She found an instructor who owned a de Havilland DH60 Moth aircraft and she was soon mastering the arts and skills required to fly an aeroplane. This was 1926, the year of the General Strike, when Abe was helping Winston Churchill and Ramsey McDonald in finding a solution to the country's misery. It hardly seemed the time to be learning to fly but Mary carried on, all the while giving what support she could to assist her husband. By now Abe knew of Mary's love for flying and did not interfere. By October 1926 Mary had attained her flying licence and had persuaded Abe to buy her a de Havilland Moth. It cost £600 which was a great deal of money in those days.

It must be said that there were relatively few registered pilots in the 1920s and precious few women. However Mary was soon into the swing of things aeronautical. She was participating in the various air shows and flying displays which were becoming popular throughout the country. She quickly won a number of prizes which showed the egotistical men around her that she was as good, and indeed better, than any of them. In 1927 Mary injured herself when swinging the propeller of her plane. But this did not put her off and though there continued to be many flying accidents, many of them ending in fatalities, she pressed on. She loved the challenges associated with her sport. Abe continued to be apprehensive about his wife every time she was flying, but Mary was not content with simply joining in the fun with the other piloting fraternity (or perhaps this should be sorority). In 1927 Mary Bailey became the first woman to fly solo over the Irish Sea. She had, if she had known it at the time, taken her first step towards greatness.

Mary was soon to set out on the air journey of a lifetime. With her husband reluctantly accepting her determination and drive and all her five children away from her at school, she felt there was nothing holding her back from achieving another first. She had a fine new plane; she had excellent flying instructors; she had the energy and ambition to undertake an air voyage of epic proportions and she had just been voted the woman aviator of the year. Now was the time to capitalise on her fame and celebrity.

On 9 March 1928 Mary Bailey set off from Stag Lane airfield north of London on the first leg of a flight which would end up in Cape Town. This was her goal but she wondered if she could achieve her ambition. She set off in a de Havilland Moth X type which she had just bought from Geoffrey de Havilland himself. It was a biplane with two seats, an open cockpit and a simple array of instruments. Into the spare seat Mary placed a couple of bags with as few belongings as possible; into the plane she brought with her only the most rudimentary maps which she had been able to acquire and she wore her favourite flying suit, goggles and helmet. This seems to us nowadays totally inadequate preparation for such a journey but, in 1928, this was all that was available and if such a flight was to be made then these were the only accoutrements to hand.

Mary safely navigated over France and Italy, making landings, of course, every few hundred miles. Fuel had always to be found as well as food and, as the journey continued, help in finding her way. Setting off from Italy, Mary flew over Sicily on her way to Malta. But she could not find this elusive Mediterranean island. Her compass was already giving bother and she had to proceed with caution. In the event she was extremely lucky to find Malta not long before her fuel tank urgently required replenishment.

Mary had made as many arrangements as she could before leaving England – where to land, who to contact and, most importantly, where to find fuel. But as she progressed the situation changed when she mostly found herself hoping and praying that she could find everything she needed in often rather primitive environments. She proceeded to fly over to Libya in north Africa and she felt proud that she had reached the continent of her final goal. It may just have been the north but she was pleased with her flight thus far. However when she reached Cairo in Egypt, Mary was confronted by her first seemingly immovable problem. She was refused permission to fly over the Sudan on her own. She could only proceed accompanied by another aviator. Her good friend, the accomplished and renowned aviator, Derek Bentley, agreed to fly along side her as she flew over those vast tracts of eastern Africa and so her journey continued.

After Bentley had left her, Mary had to make one of quite a number of semi emergency landings in the African deserts. On one occasion she had to repair a fault on her own. Her technical knowledge was limited but, as the time went on and crises mounted, Mary was able to either fix a problem herself or get someone else to do so. Once she crashed her plane on landing but fortunately she was unhurt. However the aircraft was beyond repair and she needed a new plane. Without hesitation, she cabled Abe to find another one for her. Believe it or not she immediately had a number of offers of replacements and soon had one in her possession. However she did not like this particular Moth and, after flying it to Nairobi, she was found yet another. At this stage in her journey Mary had been delayed twelve days.

Mary landed at Cape Town on 30 April 1928 after 52 days and 121 hours flying. She was met at the airfield by a much relieved Abe who hoped that his wife had got epic flights out of her system. He was about to return to England and he expected Mary to join him on a much more leisurely voyage home. But, hardly surprisingly, Mary had other ideas. She had made her mind up to fly back.

She set off on 14 May 1928 but crashed her plane soon after the start. The plane came down near Port Elizabeth when she had to make a tricky forced landing in poor weather. She quickly gave up but not before ensuring that her original Moth had been repaired and returned to her. She would start at a later date flying the aircraft which she knew best. For a number of months, with Abe back in London, Mary stayed with her friends, the van Rynevelds, on their farm in South Africa. By September she was ready to fly back to the northern hemisphere. She was strongly counselled by many not to undertake such a journey especially when she had declared that she would return by the hazardous route over west Africa this time. To return by air was going to be difficult, but to take this western tack was, to many, not so much overly ambitious, but downright crazy.

Mary's journey north

Mary took off, not from Cape Town this time, but from Pretoria on 21 September 1928. She headed for Bulawayo in Rhodesia and then flew west towards the Belgian Congo. Mary was already experiencing engine trouble so she decided to go to Luanda in Angola to have the problems rectified. This delayed her journey by a few days but she had time to get to know the country and meet people she either knew or knew about.

During her journeys Mary kept a rather basic diary. Sometimes she forgot to complete entries but, generally speaking, it did adequately reflect her experiences. Her pattern of navigation rarely changed. To find her way to her next destination, Mary had literally to peer out of her little plane and follow rivers or railways. It must be reiterated that her maps were, at best, rudimentary (like the one she had given to her by a cruise line which showed the coast of Africa as it would be seen from a luxury liner) or, at worst, non-existent. When she landed at a place she had to find an airfield if possible, locate fuel, negotiate with the local people (hoping that they were going to be friendly) to guard her plane and weigh the wings down with bags filled with sand. She then needed to find food and shelter. Amazingly throughout all those days and weeks flying over darkest Africa, Mary rarely encountered any belligerence or animosity, rather the tribes people were firstly amazed to see an aeroplane and secondly most proved to be courteous, helpful and welcoming.

Whilst the locals were kind, so the French officials in the Sahara region were unhelpful and unaccommodating. They refused Mary permission to cross the vast expanses of the desert so she decided to fly out west to the coast and continue in a northerly direction. At a place called Gao, in modern day Mali, she was stuck for two weeks waiting for fuel. This was the first time she had been held back for this reason. It is hard to believe that, even in the 1920s, there were even basic airports in most countries in Africa where the intrepid Mary could refuel. So her problems at Gao must have been very frustrating for her. Eventually she got away only to be further delayed when she broke an axle during a landing further up the coast. She got away on 16 December flying north to Dakar before having yet another forced landing in Morocco. Her engine by this time was giving a lot of trouble and she eventually limped home, having made lots of stops in Spain and France, on 17 January 1929. This time she had taken four months and 124 hours flying to arrive back in the British Isles. She was met at Stag Lane by crowds of well wishers and by her mother and two of her daughters. Unfortunately Abe was not there. He was back in South Africa suffering from ill health. But he was delighted to know that Mary was well and none the worse for her journey.

Back home
Mary had become an instant celebrity. Everyone wanted to hear of her travels into the unknown. The newspapers were full of her exploits and a number of them had kept the public informed of the progress of her marathon flight as and when they picked up news of her whereabouts. She spoke to all sorts of groups of people from all walks of life. Her fame spread throughout the land and the people of Monaghan were thrilled that a daughter of theirs was headline news. They were proud of her; the whole country was proud of her. To have travelled so far in such inhospitable

climes and to have returned virtually unscathed was a marvellous achievement. The King bestowed a DBE on Mary in the 1930 New Year's honours list. She was now a lady in her own right – Dame Mary Bailey.

For the family life was moving on. Mary was perhaps seeing a bit more of her children than she had done in their earlier lives. The truth is that her mother, Mittie, with whom Mary had never had a great relationship, had helped to keep the children together by having them with her on their school holidays and she had been a tower of strength to both Abe and Mary. As parents they were too often absent but they knew at least that their youngsters were in safe hands. Back in England they had moved out of their Bryanston Square house and during the 1930s they had two different homes in Oxfordshire. Abe, however, was very rarely in either of these houses since his health was deteriorating and he preferred to remain in South Africa.

Over the ensuing years all five Bailey children married but all their marriages ended in divorce. John Bailey (Abe's son by his first marriage) was married to Diana Churchill for a few disastrous years. One can only surmise at the reasons for the failure rate of the marital unions of the young Baileys. Perhaps it was to do with the rather unhappy childhoods which they had endured so often separated from their parents.

But Mary Bailey continued to love her addiction to flying. In these years she got to know the other famous aviatrices, Amy Johnson, Amelia Earhart and Winifred Spooner. They met from time to time and presumably discussed their daring exploits. They had every reason to do so since so many men still considered women pilots as something of an oddity. But they were anything but that carving out, as they certainly did, an aeronautical legend second to none. The names of Johnson and Earhart are still remembered today but sadly not the names of Winifred Spooner and particularly Mary Bailey.

Mary was soon making plans for another journey of discovery. She prepared to return to Cape Town to break Amy Johnson's record which had only recently beaten Mary's own time. Once more Abe and the knowledgeable flying people discouraged her but she ignored their protestations and set off in a new Puss Moth plane on 15 January 1933. This time Mary only made it to the Sahara where she had been forced to land. She decided that she had had enough and returned, rather downhearted and suffering from typhoid fever, on 14 February 1933. Her long distance flying days were over.

Mary once more fell back on horse riding which she loved. She saw more of her own family and was pleased when her brother, Richard, took up flying himself. He had surely been fired with enthusiasm for the hobby by his now famous sister. Abe, however, after a full and inspired life, was becoming more and more debilitated. He returned to have treatment in England for his arthritic condition and, sadly, he had to have one leg amputated followed, in 1938, by a further leg amputation. Nonetheless he still kept his spirits high by pursuing his lifelong interest in his stud and horse racing and by his love of politics, particularly South African politics.

He was in South Africa when World War Two broke out. His health got worse and he died at Rust-en-Vrede on 10 August 1940, aged 75. Unfortunately, due to war restrictions on travel, Mary and the children were unable to attend his funeral. He was buried in consecrated ground at the edge of his garden at his home overlooking the bay. He left most of his fortune, after seeing to the needs of his family, in trust to be spent in South Africa. Many of his fine paintings were donated to the National Gallery in Cape Town where they remain on display to this day.

Back in England Mary joined the Women's Auxiliary Air Force as a non-flyer where she gave invaluable service throughout the conflict. After the war she returned to Cape Town where she joined her son, Jim, in sorting out various aspects of Abe's will which needed clarification. In 1953 Mittie, Mary's mother, died aged 92 and Mary herself succumbed on 29 July 1960, aged almost 70. She had died from lung cancer (she had been a heavy smoker all her life) and was buried alongside Abe in the grave in the garden of their home.

Why do the Irish need to remember Mary Bailey?

Mary Westenra was an Irishwoman by birth and she remained closely bound to Ireland throughout her life. Her heart was always in Monaghan and it was at Rossmore that she learnt her particular and peculiar traits of tenacity, independence and self assurance. Her choice of spectacular hobby was a surprise to many, most notably her husband, her children and the good people of Monaghan. But she then brought fame and renown to the people and put Ireland on the map. Mary Bailey had flown the Irish Sea, the first woman ever to have done so, and she was the first woman to fly solo, in a fragile little biplane, from the British Isles to the southern tip of Africa. Mary Bailey was no ordinary woman; Mary Bailey, Irish born, ought not to be forgotten. She brought fame and honour to Ireland.

Suggested reading

1. Falloon, Jane, *Throttle Full Open – a Life of Lady Bailey, Irish Aviatrix*, Dublin, 1999.
2. Lomax, Judy, *Women of the Air*, London, 1986.
3. Naughton, Lindie, *Lady Icarus – the Life of Irish Aviator Lady Mary Heath*, Dublin, 2004.

Saidie Patterson

Courageous Champion

At the beginning of the 20th century the warren of little streets leading on to the Shankill, Falls and Woodvale Roads in Belfast housed many thousands of the city's less well off citizens. Most of the female adults, and also many of their young teenaged daughters, worked in the huge mills which covered vast swathes of land in that impoverished part of west Belfast. The houses were cramped for the large families which dwelt there; there was no such thing as an inside toilet and amenities were spartan. For these people there was little alternative to working in the mills. At least their workplace was close to their dwellings although a working day, often of twelve hours duration, left precious few moments for mothers and fathers to form decent and loving relationships with their many children. Pregnant women regularly worked until the very day of their delivery and then were expected to start again within a couple of days of the birth. If they did not get back to work quickly they would lose their jobs even if the weekly pay was but a miserable 10/- (50p) per week. The daily grind was often dangerous amidst the powerful machines in the factories; work was always dirty with the floors frequently under water and toil was nothing more than drudgery – but it had to be endured if a family was to have any chance of survival. But Belfast people were survivors even in the most trying of circumstances.

Into this rather wretched world Saidie Patterson was born on 25 November 1906 at her home at 32 Woodvale Street, a most typical of terraced mill houses close to the main thoroughfares which led into the centre of Belfast. She was the oldest of the three children of her parents, her father being a blacksmith in Harland and Wolff's shipyard. Theirs was a Methodist household in a part of the city where the majority belonged to one of the Protestant denominations.

In 1912 and at the early age of just 27, Saidie's father died and shortly afterwards Mrs Sarah Patterson remarried. Her second husband was Thomas Gracey who was a widower with five children of his own. In one fell swoop the family more than doubled in size. And soon to add to Mrs Patterson's woes was the early discovery that Thomas was suffering from a nervous disease thus meaning that he was helpless for the rest of his life. This added an incredible strain to the newly enlarged family and immediately, therefore, a great deal of extra work fell on the teenaged Saidie.

Saidie attended Woodvale National school in nearby Cambrai Street. She loved school although she had to be absent very often for she was needed at home to help look after her siblings. When she did get to school she regularly had to join the queue, known as the 'Paupers' queue', when she did not have the penny fee which was required to be paid every day. On Sundays the family attended the local Methodist church for it was imperative that everyone was seen at church often twice or three times every Sunday. There was no dodging church on the Sabbath in those days.

Working conditions

Life was hard for the working classes in Belfast and for that matter in any industrial city in those days. The 1920s were in the middle of the Depression which hit western Europe after the Great War which meant that even finding a job at a few shillings per week was a difficult proposition. A labourer might earn £1 per week and the women much less. Saidie's mother was an outworker earning less than £1 per week to prepare and fold 50 dozen linen sheets. The working day started at 6 am and even at that time children as young as eight were expected to work for at least half a day and go to school tired, cold and hungry for some hours in the afternoon. Families helped one another when they were in financial difficulties. The local pawnshop was used to tide families over until the weekend. There was little pleasure in life for anyone. It was incredibly difficult just to make ends meet.

In 1918, by which time the war was nearly over, further tragedy hit the Patterson family when Mrs Sarah Patterson died in childbirth giving life to Jean. Immediately another young mouth needed to be fed with no mother to give the child sustenance. Saidie, only just 12 years old, had to bear the main burden of looking after her many siblings because her stepfather was incapable of giving any assistance in his paralysed condition. But a gallant Saidie somehow managed to survive these additional burdens and prospered as best she could.

Soon Saidie was working at the gigantic William Ewart and Son's mill. She had to work from 6 am until 6 pm with a short break in the middle of the day to run home and care for the family. The irony was that she and her hundreds of fellow workers were preparing the finest Irish linen for wealthy customers elsewhere in the ill-divided world and yet they had to eat their own packed lunches off newspapers laid out on their work benches. As Saidie looked around, therefore, she could see the hardships and dangers faced daily by those who worked in these immense buildings. Many were injured in the course of their hazardous occupation which meant that they would not only lose their job but would also lose their 'tied' house. If you could not pay your rent – even if you had been injured in the factory – then you were thrown out of your home. Disease, too, was rife and this caused concern amongst the workforce. You could easily become infected through no fault of your own.

Saidie Patterson decided that enough was enough. She had been threatened with the sack from her job for helping a colleague who was in difficulty. This would have been disastrous for her family as they relied on her pay to keep the home intact. She went to face the Ewart's director in the lion's den and described her workmates' dire work situation. She had done something never attempted before. Female workers didn't go to the bosses. But, for Saidie, this was a matter of principle for if a worker had a reasonable grievance then he or she should be able to air it without fear of losing their job. Saidie won her case and kept her job. And she had achieved something else by taking her stand. She had set a precedent enabling future disputes to be discussed with the bosses. Consequently Saidie became a focal point for others with difficulties with the firm. Her guts and perseverance had won the day.

Working for the mill girls

Saidie was a very special young woman. It has been seen that she worked extremely hard to keep her family together; she had worked immensely hard to fight for the rights of her colleagues at work. Now she was determined to work even harder for her friends to give them at least some of the opportunities experienced by better off residents of Belfast. Recreation, education and holidays were almost totally unknown for working class girls. Saidie clearly saw a need to offer them something to lift their lives out of drudgery. So she involved herself in the Belfast Girls' Club Union and in various classes for the girls in church halls close to her home. She was even able to find short holiday breaks for them in the seaside resorts of Bangor and Portrush. This gave all of them a boost and meant that they could return to work and their families with some added vigour.

The most important involvement for Saidie now came in the shape of campaigning for better working conditions for mill workers. Her early skirmish with the directors at Ewart's had given her a great deal of confidence. If the men could belong to trades unions then, decided Saidie, so could women. She knew that they also needed the protection of their own trade union so that her colleagues could work under those improved conditions. As a leader, Saidie Patterson was a natural. If anyone was going to defend women's rights, she was the one. But it had to be remembered that there was a great depression in Belfast as elsewhere. Upwards of 25% of the population was out of work. Northern Ireland had greater difficulties than Great Britain and the rates of poverty were higher here than in any other part of the United Kingdom.

But Saidie worked on. Apart from the Depression, she had two other massive obstacles. One she could have expected, but not so the other. She knew that she would meet opposition from the employers for they obviously wanted to make their healthy profits without having to be bothered with improving pay and conditions for their workers. But she had not reckoned with the other problem. This came from the men workers. They had their own unions and powerful trades unionists by now but, when they heard of Saidie's campaign to improve women's circumstances, they baulked at the thought of having to share their hard-won improved benefits with their women colleagues. In the end, although she had to fight her corner, Saidie's tenacity triumphed. The mill girls of Belfast had found their champion.

The Second World War

As the storm clouds gathered over Europe it seemed evident that there would soon be a conflict of mighty proportions. It was also clear that the Belfast mills would be required to provide various necessary supplies to prosecute the war. This was the time for the women to take a firm stand and Saidie, although appreciating the seriousness of a war situation, knew that this was the moment to make sure her women had a decent pay compared with the men and, more importantly, to keep pay differentials as narrow as possible. The bosses would ignore the power of their women workers at their peril; they would need the vast army of mill girls to produce many vital materials for the war effort. Two male trades union stalwarts now made close friendships with Saidie – in England none other than Ernest Bevin and, in Belfast, Bob Getgood. They realised the clout that women had in the workplace and appreciated their importance. They also clearly saw the inspiration which Saidie was showing to her women and earmarked her for promotion in their respective trades unions. Bevin's union backed Saidie and encouraged her in her push for women's recognition at Ewart's. The crux of the matter for Saidie was whether or not the men would support their female colleagues should they go on strike. She insisted on this condition and they rather reluctantly agreed. But Saidie's next problem was to get the women to join the trade union. Many of them were apprehensive for they thought that if they did join, then their homes might be at risk from vindictive employers. There were many meetings held at Saidie's home until, at last, the majority of women agreed with her plan.

The big strike
Deep down Saidie only considered organising a strike with a heavy heart. She realised that the war was on and the Allies needed every piece of linen that Ewart's produced. But even deeper down Saidie knew that this was her chance, once and for all, to attain equal benefits and a more reasonable pay for the women workers. By late 1939, not long after the start of the conflict, Saidie and her union faced up the directors at Ewart's. There did not seem much of a chance for a compromise and a strike seemed to loom large on the horizon. But Saidie was ready. She had cast aside her gremlins and was prepared to take her stand. The firm was happy enough for the workers to join Saidie's union, but she insisted on 100% membership to ensure that every one of the girls would accept the consequences of their actions. The management would not agree to this and so the strike was called for the end of February 1940. Nearly 2,000 women went on strike with the full support of unions everywhere. The union promised 12/- (60p) per week strike pay which would only have kept a family on the most frugal fare. Ewart's tried moral blackmail something which Saidie knew was a probability. The firm needed to be supplying materials for a war – did the workers forget this? They did not and were saddened that they had been forced to take this action.

Throughout the seven week strike Saidie came into her own as a public speaker. There were many, of course, who condemned the action but she spoke up and told her often critical audiences the reasons for having taken such a drastic stance. Her listeners drew in their horns when they heard of the conditions under which the mill women had been working. Saidie became very well known and was invited to address many gatherings for the duration of the strike. The public, only then beginning to appreciate the realities of the virtual slave labour conditions in the mills, fell in behind Saidie and contributed generously to the strike fund so much so that strike pay was increased to 16/- (80p) per week.

After these seven weeks Saidie, although she had not actually gained all she had wanted, agreed that the women should return to their machines. They had been encouraged to go back by the big trade union leaders both in London and Belfast. The women had certainly made their mark, gaining the respect of so many people throughout Northern Ireland. Women in other places of work benefited from the action of Saidie and her ladies and they were grateful for that. Improvements were gradually implemented in the mills not only with an increase in pay, a major victory, but also the introduction of some paid holidays.

Before the war was over Saidie became a fulltime official for the textile branch of the Transport Union in Belfast but, most importantly, employers now knew not to ignore their female employees again. In fact the vast majority of mill owners quickly introduced these improved conditions under which the women worked. Had it not been for Saidie Patterson, however, it would have taken much longer for them to improve the lot of their embattled women employees.

Saidie – the Trade Union official

When the Ewart's strike was ended Saidie now moved into the world of the trades unions. Her primary concern was always to concentrate on conditions for women. In this she succeeded. By now, she was beginning to meet, and work with, the great and good amongst the Labour union fraternity. At home she not only nurtured her relationship with Bob Getgood but also got to know another official, William Walker, who was very much a self taught man. With her links with Bevin in England Saidie was now meeting the likes of Clement Attlee, soon to become the post-war Prime Minister, Winston Churchill and other prominent men in government. She became a member of the Standing Conference of Women's Organisations which fought constantly for better health and welfare conditions for women and their families. Health conditions in Northern Ireland quickly improved and child mortality, for example, was greatly reduced from previously unacceptably high levels.

Involvement with politics

As soon as the war was over the 1945 General Election was held. If the tough Mr Churchill thought his war deeds, great and courageous as they were, were going to result in the return of a Conservative government by a grateful people, he was to be sadly mistaken. The Labour party, under Clement Attlee, was elected with a huge overall majority. And in Northern Ireland, the Prime Minister, Sir Basil Brooke, had also called a General Election. Saidie set about with her usual determination to help Northern Ireland Labour Party representatives to be returned to Stormont. Her hard work for Bob Getgood in the Oldpark constituency paid off when he was elected with another three NILP candidates. However, despite her hard work in the 1949 election, Getgood failed to be returned.

Saidie, whose commitment to the Labour cause was almost legendary, was elected treasurer of the Northern Ireland Labour Party in 1950 and then further, in 1956, elected to the supreme position of party chairman. Her work for the party is seen, to this very day, as a unifying force for the people of Northern Ireland. In the 1958 General Election, when Brooke (now Lord Brookeborough) was still Prime Minister, there was resurgence for the NILP and, once more, four candidates won seats in Stormont. Vivian Simpson was by now the Oldpark representative and, much to Saidie's delight, he was elected again with three other candidates. Four MPs for the Northern Ireland Labour Party was to be their maximum number at any election in the 50 years of the Province's own parliament.

During Captain Terence O'Neill's incumbency as Prime Minister from 1963 until 1969, the fortunes of the NILP took a battering. O'Neill showed a steely determination to curtail the rising influence of the NILP and managed to crush their hopes and aspirations at the 1965 election when just two NILP MPs were elected. The party's powerbase was slipping away and they were never able to regain their previous position of achived in 1945 and 1958. Despite Saidie's best endeavours the party was on the wane. She continued to advocate membership of the non sectarian NILP but, with the 'Troubles' looming, she encountered little success.

Northern Ireland slips into the abyss

Saidie Patterson was probably one of the first perceptive people in Northern Ireland to see the deep-rooted problems which were affecting the Province. She knew that sectarianism would tear the place apart and she did what she could to try to foster good community relations. She truly believed that membership of the Northern Ireland Labour Party would help contribute to a less strained society but she was unfortunately defeated in her attempts to improve life in a troubled society. By the 1960s she had retired from the Transport Union. Her hard work in the mills and for the fortunes of the NILP had had some successes but also some setbacks. As well as involving herself in election activities at regular intervals, Saidie espoused the Moral Rearmament cause and met many friends in that organisation who were to remain close to her throughout the rest of her life.

By the early 1970s the Northern Ireland troubles had firmly caught hold. Saidie joined the Women Together organisation, a group of mainly working class women under the leadership of Ruth Agnew and Monica Patterson. Their aim was to support women in the most vulnerable parts of Belfast who were facing terror and hardship every day. Saidie was, as ever, the backbone of this organisation and became their chairman shortly after the fall of Stormont in the spring of 1972. She ensured that the women and their children who needed the most help received it and arranged holidays for them to take them away from the stress and strain of life in a very disturbed city. Saidie became more and more proficient as a speaker and her presence was requested in every corner of the world. She made speech after speech trying to make people understand the utter futility of sectarian strife. She had some successes especially when local politicians, not normally given to listening to the voice of the people, stood back and paid heed to Saidie's entreaties. She was often asked to go to meetings organised by them to try to talk sense into audiences not normally given to listening to good advice.

In 1979, by which time she was 73 years old, Saidie was invited to give an oration for peace in St Patrick's Cathedral, Dublin during the visit to Ireland by Pope John Paul II. How Saidie Patterson had changed from the early days of her life trying to make ends meet for her large family and improving working conditions for women in the Belfast mills.

The Peace People

When the young relatives of Mairead Corrigan were killed in a tragic stolen car incident in August 1976, the resultant public outpouring of support turned into the Peace People. There was huge cross-community support for this movement which was led by Mairead Corrigan and Betty Williams with, as could be expected, willing assistance from Saidie Patterson. It was she who organised a march up Belfast's Shankill Road for members of both communities on Saturday 28 August 1976. It was an outstanding success with over 50,000 Catholic and Protestant women completing their walk in Woodvale Park. Saidie addressed the assembled crowds and hit all the right notes in what she had to say. This most complex and difficult march had gone extremely well, so much so that a similar gathering was organised for the Falls Road soon afterwards. Sadly this march was broken up by hooligan stone throwers who caused many injuries to the marchers. Saidie herself was badly injured and was only saved from further distress by a number of the local Catholic women. She had to spend many weeks in hospital with a spinal injury although when she was eventually discharged she is reported as saying that 'at least my tongue has not been affected'. But for Saidie her marching days and much of her work for the people were over.

Saidie's legacy

Saidie Patterson was a woman of the people. She knew their difficulties and woes for she herself had also suffered them. In her later years she was honoured by every organisation and university. She was awarded the Joseph Parker Peace Prize in 1977, the same year that her own Methodist Church presented her with their Peace Prize. For this woman who had only received a patchy National School education she must have been very proud when the Open University conferred on her an honorary degree. But, probably best of all for Saidie, was when the Women's International League for Peace and Freedom named her in the world's top 100 distinguished women for 1975. Saidie Patterson had climbed many mountains and jumped over many hurdles to improve the rights of women in the Belfast mills; Saidie Patterson had fought to encourage ordinary Belfast citizens to join the non sectarian Northern Ireland Labour party; Saidie Patterson had shown by her example what peace could bring to a Province which so desperately needed it. In the end whilst Saidie had succeeded in some of her endeavours and failed in others, she had shown a sceptical population that she meant business. When she died in 1985, aged 78, Northern Ireland was most certainly a better place for having experienced the grit and determination of such a wonderfully courageous woman as Woodvale's own Saidie Patterson.

Suggested reading

1.   Bleakley, David, *Saidie Patterson – Irish Peacemaker*, Belfast, 1980.